OUT OF THE FLAME

The Harold Chalfant Story
by Capitola Gwillim

Published by

THE WORD FOR TODAY

Presented To: _____

From: _____

Date: _____

A Keepsake Edition
In Loving Memory of Harold George Chalfant

March 18, 1913 – January 18, 1989
"For me to live is Christ, and to die is gain."

Philippians 1:21

ACKNOWLEDGMENTS

The Harold Chalfant Memorial Camp Committee:
Don Stauffer, Jerry Jensen, Roy McKeown, Allan Lamb,
Dean Miller, and Leonard Harvey.
Photography – Don Stauffer

Invaluable Contributions:
Joyce Chalfant Bevers
Marlayn Stauffer
Gladys Bell
Nadine Camp
Paul Chalfant
Ruby Chalfant
Edythe Dorrance
Bob Freeman
Roy Lane
John Littlefield
Rolf K. McPherson
Helen Jensen

Special thanks go to Charles "Chuck" Smith, Barney
Northcote, and so many of the members of the circle of
friends for their dedication and gifts to make this project
possible.

The missionary segment part III includes revised excerpts
from "Through Green Hell on an Ox" written by Harold
Chalfant, 1938.

Published by **The Word For Today** 1994
P.O. Box 8000 Costa Mesa CA 92628
ISBN 0–936728–51–5

Table of Contents

PART I
A MINISTRY TO YOUTH

DEDICATION

Out Of The Flame is dedicated to the perpetuation of the vision of Christian summer camps, worldwide in emphasis, in a united effort to influence our boys and girls in the formative stages of their lives, and to introduce them to the all–sufficient One, our Lord and Savior Jesus Christ.

Further, our purpose is to instill within young hearts and minds a sound knowledge of Bible–oriented principles which, through the agency of the Holy Spirit, will change and challenge their lives, shaping destinies for now, and all eternity.

Dr. Roy B. McKeown
President
World Opportunities International
Hollywood, California

PREFACE

Harold Chalfant was the first Sunday School teacher who impacted me following my commitment to Jesus Christ. In 1935, at the age of 19, I went to Hollywood, seeking a career in motion pictures, a desire I had since I was ten and a member of a traveling vaudeville troupe.

Early in my 20th year, I was introduced to Christ by one who had a background in the Foursquare Church and knew Harold Chalfant. As pastor of Vermont Avenue Presbyterian Church, he wanted to start a college class, and Harold Chalfant was our first teacher – I might add, an unforgettable teacher. As one new in his pilgrimage with Christ, I was profoundly impressed by this man... his love for Christ which was so contagious, his knowledge of the Scriptures which was so illuminating, his marvelous spontaneity and humor were just what I needed as a recent convert.

There is a sense in which, apart from my pastor who led me to Christ, Harold Chalfant had the most definitive influence on my life in those formative years. My memory of him is a blessed one, and "I thank my God upon every remembrance" of Harold Chalfant.

Richard C. Halverson, DD.
Chaplain
United States Senate

INTRODUCTION

"This is the amazing story of an outstanding young man who rose far above his natural circumstances to influence the lives of thousands of young people throughout the world. His challenge to live recklessly for God brought forth leaders who had a tremendous influence at home and abroad. His dauntless faith and adventuresome strides greatly inspired his generation.

I counted Harold Chalfant as a great personal friend and co–worker in the work of the Lord. His contributions to the youth program of the International Church of the Foursquare Gospel were tremendous and his camping achievements still live on in the lives of countless numbers of young people today."

Rolf K. McPherson, DD.
President Emeritus
International Church of the
Foursquare Gospel

PART I
A MINISTRY TO YOUTH

CHAPTER 1
HIS LIFE TOUCHED MINE

His life touched mine,
Mine is touching others
And so the ripples go out
Around the world.

A ripple from the life of Harold Chalfant is touching your life today as you read this book. Within these pages is recounted the ministry and influence Harold had on the lives of hundreds of thousands of young people around the world.

You will read many accounts of those who testify to the dynamic affect Harold's ministry had on their lives. None are any more dramatic than that of Pastor Chuck Smith of the Calvary Chapel in Costa Mesa, California.

To introduce you to the life and legend of Harold Chalfant, here, in his own words, is the story of how Harold's life touched that of Pastor Chuck Smith...

As a young man my great love was the beach and I was planning another exciting summer at Corona Del Mar, California.

My plans changed abruptly on a beautiful Sunday morning in church. At the conclusion of the worship services, my pastor asked me if I wanted to go to summer camp at Camp Radford, Located in the San Bernardino Mountains. I wasn't very interested, even though I had grown up in Foursquare Churches and had heard of their summer camps.

My pastor informed me that a person in the church had given a scholarship for someone who wanted to go, and if I was willing he could arrange to have someone come to Redlands, pick me up and take me there. Since a free "anything" was always hard for me to pass up, I told him if he could make the arrangements for me, I'd go.

Early the next morning with my sleeping bag and suitcase in hand, I boarded a bus and rode out from Santa Ana to Redlands. How little I knew then that in the providence of God's wisdom, Jesus would be waiting at this camp to reveal Himself as Lord of my life. How little I knew then that this new experience with Christ would change the destiny of my life.

Promptly at noon, a car drove up to the Carnation Malt Shop in Redlands. The driver called out, "Are you Chuck Smith? I'm Harold Chalfant."

He invited me to jump into the back seat of his car. I'll never forget the ride up the mountain. The tires were squealing around the curves, as we sped up the hill. "This guy is really cool!" I thought. He talked a lot about camp and what was going on up there. I was immediately taken with him.

At this time in my life I was taking courses heavy in science, in keeping with my ambition to become a neurosurgeon. I had seriously begun to doubt the Bible story of creation, as I was being exposed to the evolutionary theory. Even though my parents were very committed Christians, I was at a turning point in my life. I was being weaned from their faith, and beginning to develop my own.

We arrived at camp in time for afternoon sports. I was asked to play baseball on the Santa Monica team, and immediately got into the swing of things.

That night Harold led worship during Victory Circle. As I listened to the testimonies from the campers something incredibly beautiful was happening to me. On that unforgettable night God began a wondrous work in my life. Unknown to me, the Lord had brought me up to camp that He might become more than just my Savior. Jesus wanted to become the Lord of my life.

Harold inspired me to completely commit my life to Jesus Christ. No other person had done that before. I remember him saying, "We only have one life, and it will soon be past; and only what's done for Christ will last." That made sense to me.

As a result, the Lord began dealing with my heart. I sensed the Holy Spirit saying, "If you give your life to medicine, you will be able to help people, but at best the help will be temporary. There is a deadly malady that is plaguing mankind called sin. If you give your life to healing man from this plague, the results will be eternal. Do you want to devote your life to things which are temporal, or to things which are eternal?"

The next morning as I sat in Harold's Science and the Bible class, I began to get answers to the questions that had brought so much doubt and confusion to my mind. I thought, "This guy knows more about science than any of my teachers and what he's saying really makes sense." The class brought me into a tremendous appreciation of just how great God really is. I was excited! I was animated with a clearer understanding of the person of Jesus Christ! At that point I became a committed Christian.

I'll never forget another part of camp called "Skit Night". I can still see Harold wearing a pair of giant shoes. Then he baked a cake on Ulphin Davis' head. I never laughed so much in all of my life. That's when I realized that Christians can laugh and have fun.

That was the beginning of a wonderful relationship with a man whom God used in my life to inspire me to become a "fool for Christ." As Harold often said, "You're a fool for someone; you might as well become a fool for Christ."

The last night during Victory Circle, I threw my pine cone into the fire as a token of my commitment to Christ. As I stood there at the fire pit, I was forever changed by the marvelous power of the Holy Spirit, who used a man named Harold Chalfant to challenge me to totally commit my life to Christ. I stood at the invitation for all of those who were willing to respond to God's call to go to Bible College in preparation for the ministry.

I went back to my home church and really began to get involved in the youth program, becoming the Crusader President. (In the Foursquare Church the young people's group was called Crusaders.) The next year I brought over one hundred of my friends with me to camp desiring that they too might receive the same inspiration that this man of God had brought to me.

When I enrolled in Bible School, I would hang around the Crusader office just to be near Harold. He was so gracious to me. He asked me to help him put flagstone in his back yard, then we dug out a basement in his home. I'll never forget the night we put up the metal laths over the studs in the new basement. The black flecks from the metal completely covered our faces.

As we sat at the dinner table looking at each other, we started laughing at ourselves. It was hilarious. I was sitting with my hero. I had become close to him. We were working together, eating together, laughing together. I was as close to heaven as any teenager could be.

Harold began giving me opportunities to work with him at camp. On one of the trips we took together, we walked over the raw acreage of what was to become Camp Cedar Crest. With panoramic vision, Harold pointed out where the swimming pool, ball diamond, dining hall and chapel would eventually be built. The entire time we worked together to make his vision a reality, he was continuing to inspire, challenge and shape my life.

God brought another great inspiration into my life when He gave me my wife, Kay. I had been praying and looking for this girl all of my life. When we became engaged I told her that I wanted Harold Chalfant to perform the wedding ceremony. In front of the fireplace in the living room of the Chalfant home on Kensington Road in Los Angeles, we were married. God blessed me again beyond my wildest dreams when He gave me Kay, my wonderful wife.

I caught the vision from Harold to serve the Lord working among youth and developing summer camps. Through the ministry of Calvary Chapel we have been blessed to see tens of thousands of young people come to Jesus Christ and commit their lives to Christian service. We also have built a summer camp situated on 400 acres, located very near to the Foursquare camp. How we praise the Lord for the privilege of ministering to the needs of so many today!

The passionate vision Harold Chalfant passed on to me was passed on to the present generation, and now to the next generation. I remember Harold saying that when a pebble is thrown into a pond, that the ripples continue going out further and further and you never know where they will reach. I will be forever thankful to the Lord for bringing Harold Chalfant into my life.

> His life touched mine,
> Mine is touching others
> And so the ripples go out
> Around the world.

Charles "Chuck" Smith
Pastor Calvary Chapel
Costa Mesa, California

CHAPTER 2
FAMILY ROOTS

In the Chalfant family archives there is a faded letter preserved, dated: August 23, 1921. It is a letter written to a friend by N.B. Chalfant, son of John Chalfant:

"In the old Hugenot graveyard between Philadelphia and Germantown, Pennsylvania there stands an old tombstone on which is written: Edward Chalfant, Enrique Franciamont, 1775. Translated into English, it means, Edward Chalfant, refugee from France, died 1775. I could not discern more on the stone, as it had been badly chipped by British bullets."

"It is supposed that Edward was on a ship loaded with Hugenots who sailed from England in 1735 and settled near Philadelphia, Pennsylvania. They built a church and of course, a graveyard.

"Lafayette took refuge in this stone church with a few men in his fight with Lord Howe at Germantown; the British battered it down to rubble. The church was never rebuilt, but the graveyard is filled on about an acre of land. Few of the graves were under 100 years old in 1875. This is the first record of a Chalfant in America.

"Two boys, David and Chad, fought in the Continental army. Although very young, they fought in the battle of Brandywine. After the army was discharged at Trenton, New York, my grandfather Chalfant rode on a horse over the mountains behind an officer and stopped where Brownstown now stands, 25 miles from Pittsburgh on the Monogenla River. He lived there until he died. His body lies buried under the pulpit of the Methodist Church in Brownstown.

"All the Chalfants in the West originated from his lineage. He had six sons and one daughter; David, William, Robert, Mordicia, Abner, Walter and Elizabeth. Abner, my father, settled in Tuscarawas County, Ohio in 1812. I am the only living member of his family. My brothers and sister died without issue. Uncle Robert settled in Guernsey County in 1813. He was the daddy of all the Chalfants in Ohio. He had a large family of boys who settled all over the West."

WHEN A CHILD IS BORN

One son who settled in the West was George Chalfant. He settled in Clovis, New Mexico, the population then being around 5,000, but today is approximately 20,000. He married Nora Doyle, of Scotch–Irish descent from Southern Tennessee. There were six sons born into the home of Nora and George Chalfant the yougest was Harold George Chalfant, born March 18 1913.

Many times Harold was heard to say, "Both of my parents were devout Christian people. Dad, by his daily example, demonstrated all that a good father should be. Mother was the cohesive force that kept our family together."

Harold often said, "I believe the Lord had a plan for my life, a niche to fill."

> *"Before I formed you in the belly, I knew you; and before you came forth out of the womb I sanctified you, and ordained you a prophet unto the nation."* (Jeremiah 1:5)

After he had grown up and dedicated his life to Christ, he learned from his mother there was no way he could have done anything else but preach the Gospel. "No way!" he often said, "My destiny was beyond the control of man."

After Harold was born, the youngest of six sons, his little mother held him in her arms and presented him to the Lord, praying, "Lord, I give my baby son to You for the ministry." Intensely and with great emotion between sobs, he would say, "I couldn't have done anything else!"

MAKING THE RIGHT DECISION

In 1925, a sudden crisis changed the future of the Chalfant family...

Harold's father, George Chalfant, was a self–taught electrical engineer. He personally installed the first power plant in Clovis, New Mexico, bringing light to 185 homes. He held the position of city manager for 17 years.

When a big eastern company came to Clovis to install electrical generators for the city, the work was done in an improper manner. "Dad" Chalfant was offered a $50,000 bribe to close his eyes to the slipshod work and forget that any problems existed. He refused to compromise with the corrupt politicians and as a result lost his position with the city. This set–back broke his heart. And so it was that at the age of 45, George Chalfant had to start his career all over again, with no prospects of another position in view. In the throes of critical economic conditions, Nora and George Chalfant sold everything they owned, and moved West with their family.

ON ROUTE 66

In a model–T Ford California bound, the family traveled on Route 66. It took several days to arrive in Los Angeles, their desired destination. This kind of trip required a tremendous leap of faith! They turned their many problems over to the Lord and sought His mind for guidance. In the midst of these trials, Harold's mother and father continued to believe that, "...*all things work together for good to them that love God, to them who are the called according to His purpose."* (Romans 8:28)

God honored their child–like faith. They encountered just about every form of opposition one can imagine, including intense heat, flash floods, flat tires and sudden storms. Through it all, however, they managed to enjoy the magnificent petrified forest and the awe–inspiring Grand Canyon. Harold always felt that good parents were a heritage from the Lord. He always thanked the Lord for his wonderful parents.

THE ADOLESCENCE OF A MAN

Paul Chalfant, three years older than Harold, gives a brief glimpse of his and Harold's relationship as siblings...

"Doctors had diagnosed Harold as having a heart irregularity. Parental orders were that he was not to have any older brother corrections, consequently he was spoiled – in fact, a pain.

"As a pre–teen and on through high school when he was 'Big Man on Campus', his personality showed absolutely no improvement. In my opinion, he was still a pain. Clearly, even then, he showed unusual talent in winning the favor of people. He became the long time friend and protegé of his high school principal, Mr. Bengani. He excelled in sports – particularly baseball and swimming. I am proud to have had him as my brother. We were very fortunate to have had a Mother and Dad who taught us the most important issues of life."

GREEN SALAD DAYS OF YOUTH

When the Chalfant family moved from Clovis, New Mexico to Los Angeles, Harold was twelve years of age. He lived in the same neighborhood for sixty years. He went to grammar school and Thomas Starr King Junior High School in the Silver Lake District. He attended Belmont High School, located at Beverly and Second Street. The student enrollment then was 900. Today it is recognized as one of the largest high schools in the country with an enrollment of over 4,800.

CHAPTER 3
ANGELUS TEMPLE

Angelus Temple was the epicenter of Harold's life... his church home. The church seated 5,000 people and was filled to capacity for every service. For years young Harold never sat in a seat during church. All the kids had to sit on the steps of the third balcony.

Harold remembered, "On Sunday mornings, I'd see thousands of people lined up outside, waiting for the doors to open. It would be filled in ten minutes. But the same thing happened on Sunday afternoon and evening, too. Multitudes of people would line up from Echo Park Avenue to Sunset Boulevard. After service, they would empty the church for an hour, preparing for the afternoon service – Then unbelievably It would be filled again for the evening service. The people would start lining up at 4:00 p.m."

On Friday evenings, the young people were in charge. Hubert Mitchell was their leader. Again, over 5,000 young people would pack into the auditorium, its vaulted ceilings designed to simulate the sky and heavenly regions above the earth. A 75 year old woman painted the dome while lying on her back, supported by scaffolding. It was reputed to be the largest unsupported dome of its kind in North America.

Every day of the week, Monday through Saturday, services were held with three services on Sunday. In conjunction with this heavy schedule, there were always morning and afternoon services held in adjoining meeting rooms. Harold's spiritual life was nourished and enriched by having been a part of this phenomenal outpouring of the Holy Spirit.

Clearly, God had His hand upon Harold Chalfant during his formative years, although he had not yet fully surrendered his life to Christ. Imperceptibly, however, events kept happening which ultimately would change his life forever...

When Harold's mother began attending Angelus Temple, she made sure Harold and his brother Robert accompanied her. At the age of 12, Harold accepted Jesus Christ as his personal Savior, through the anointed ministry of Aimee Semple McPherson, founder of the International Church of the Foursquare Gospel. He considered Mrs. McPherson the most influential person in shaping the destiny of his life.

THE CLARION CALL

Soon after his conversion, Harold had a very unusual experience which left an indelible imprint upon his future life. One night while sleeping, he believed that an angel of the Lord called him by name. Startled and confused from sleep, he got up and went into his mother's room, thinking she had called him. She hadn't, so he went back to bed. After he had fallen asleep, he heard his name called a second time. There was no plausible explanation. In puzzled wonderment he went back to sleep a third time. In a short while he heard his name being spoken again. This time he bolted out of bed, got his Bible and began reading from Isaiah 43:1,2. Needless to say this passage impacted him with the awesome reality of God's sovereignty:

*"...I have called [thee] by thy name; thou art Mine. When thou
passest through the waters, I will be with thee; and through the
rivers, they shall not overflow thee: when thou walkest through
the fire, thou shalt not be burned; neither shall the flame kindle
upon thee."* (Isaiah 43:1-2)

The call was like a gentle whisper, with the sensation of
warm breath upon his ear. It was too real to ignore.

A man named Dr. A. P. Gouthey came to Angelus Temple to
hold a revival campaign. His academic resume included 14
years of university training, majoring in the sciences. He was
not only intellectually astute but spiritually sensitive to the
things of God as well. Harold was captivated by his pulpit ora-
tory. He was most effective as a Bible expositor. His gentility,
humility and humanity appealed enormously to Harold as a
young man in search of truth. The campaign lasted 12 weeks.
At the close of the meeting, Harold made a complete dedication of his life to the Lord.

Dr. Clarence Hall was Angelus Temple's first Crusader
Youth president. As a youth motivator, he inspired consecrat-
ed leadership. Harold's first interest in youth began with Dr.
Hall.

The youth services were fantastic. The energy level was
consistently high from the music to the passionate preaching
of the Word. It was during those times that Harold first discovered the power and anointing of God upon his ministry.

*"...Who hath saved us, and called us with an holy calling, not
according to our works, but according to His own purpose and
grace, which was given us in Christ Jesus before the world
began..."* (II Timothy 1:9)

Clarence Hall explains it this way:

"Harold Chalfant received Jesus Christ as his Savior and
Lord in Angelus Temple in 1932. He began attending our
Youth Crusader services Sunday afternoons on the fourth
floor of L.I.F.E. Bible College building. When we discovered
this unusual and outstanding young man, Elsie Edland (who

later became his wife) and I felt we should introduce him to our group. We did not know his full name, so Elsie said, 'Let's just call him Harold.'

"Soon afterwards I asked Harold to join the group that conducted meetings each Sunday evening on the corner of Alvarado and Seventh streets in Los Angeles. He was hesitant, but finally agreed to do so, providing I would assure him that he would not have to speak.

"Neglecting to keep my promise, I presented Harold to the crowd gathered on that corner. He took the challenge and stepped to the curbside to give his first public testimony of faith in Jesus Christ. Although nervous, he continued to speak even when two girls he recognized from his high school came by. He often said that this experience, being pressured to speak publicly, launched him into his preaching ministry.

"Harold attended our Crusader prayer meetings in the "120 Room" Monday nights where we gathered to wait on the Lord for His fullness. God met him there as he prayed, and he became divinely equipped and anointed for his incomparable ministry, reaching people of all ages with his amazing sermons filled with tremendous facts, figures, missionary experiences and Bible knowledge.

"In June 1934, when I resigned from the position of Crusader Leader at Angelus Temple, Harold was chosen to fill this position by Aimee Semple McPherson. During a Thanksgiving Breakfast at Clifton's downtown cafeteria, he challenged the Foursquare young people to begin a summer camp program in the mountain area of Southern California. From this came the Cedar Crest camp near running springs. Harold knew the mountains so well. He loved them and hiked many hundreds of miles through great portions of the area he had become very familiar with. In the development of Cedar Crest, Harold gave himself unsparingly. His vision became a reality."

Oh Turn Me, Mold Me

Oh, turn me, mold me, mellow me for use
Pervade my being with thy vital force
That this else inexpressive life of mine
May become eloquent and full of power,
Impregnated with life and strength divine
Put the bright torch of heaven in my hand,
That I may carry it aloft
And win the eye of weary wanderers here below
To guide their feet in the paths of peace
I cannot raise the dead,
Nor from this soil pluck precious dust,
Nor bid the sleeper wake,
Nor still the storm, nor bend the lightning back,
Nor muffle up the thunder,
Nor bid the chains fall from off the creations long
enfettered limbs
But I can live a life that tells on other lives,
And make this world less full of anguish and pain;
A life that like the pebble dropped upon the sea
Sends its wide circles to a hundred shores
May such a life be mine
Creator of true life, Thyself the life Thou givest,
Give Thyself, that thou mayest dwell in me, and I in Thee.

Horatius Bonar

CHAPTER 4
IN PREPARATION

Restless, reckless, resolute and revolutionary. In their proper perspective, these adjectives fit Harold Chalfant well, but there is another word which perhaps more aptly characterizes him. The word is "real", as in genuine. In his youth he was like a diamond in the rough, with tremendous possibilities for polish and refinement.

In many ways, Harold's character brings to mind James' assessment of Elijah, "a man of like passions". He was not an angel or some super spiritual being, but a man who was mightily used by God. He possessed an innate curiosity toward the phenomena of the material world. The wonders of the great outdoors fascinated him. Little wonder that he was irresistibly drawn to the call of nature and the mysteries of the physical universe about him.

LONELY CROSSROADS
As a loner, he spent much of his time in the mountains devouring the wonders of the universe around him. About this time he began to drift away from God. Perhaps his spiritual zeal was dimmed by getting his eyes on people with all their disconcerting imperfections. Perhaps he wanted to escape

from the pressures of life and feel safe and secure in the solitude of the mountains.

During Harold's mid–teens he contemplated pursuing a secular vocation. Just before he enrolled as a student at L. I. F. E. Bible College to prepare for the ministry, he took a trip north and enrolled in classes at the University of Washington:

"I wanted to study log engineering," he said, "where I could either work for a private logging company or for the government."

What he had in mind was becoming a park ranger, possibly working at Yosemite, Yellowstone National Park or the Grand Canyon. The outdoors was in his blood. He loved it!

"Looking back," he continued, "I can see how the Lord had His finger upon my life because He certainly gave me an abundance of outdoor work, with summer camps and missions, too. It was marvelous to spend entire summers in the Rockies, or eastern Canada, or on the Columbia River, or in the San Bernardino Mountains."

Harold most decidedly had traveling in his blood. Since 1932 he wore out 51 automobiles, vans and pick–up trucks. The Foursquare organization gave him an international card which entitled him the rare privilege to travel on any airline in the entire world, at any time. Additionally, with annual passes, God opened the doors for him to travel on the Southern Pacific, Union Pacific and the Santa Fe train lines, free of charge.

God granted him the desires of his heart. For a while Harold thought his life would be restricted to one confined area, but the Lord made it possible for him to see the world. Indeed, the world became his parish. Harold never forgot the faithfulness of God in allowing him to serve in this capacity.

SPHERE OF INFLUENCE

The value of a child held great significance for Harold Chalfant. He recognized the importance of parochial training for the young. His own life was influenced by Sunday School and Vacation Bible School, two important arms of the church.

One summer he desperately wanted to attend Vacation Bible School, but there was no money. It was during The Great Depression days and everybody was struggling just to survive. Harold said, "I remember so well a special lady at Angelus Temple who was willing to take a chance on me. She offered to sponsor my tuition for two weeks. Her loving gesture of concern touched me very much. I mean, she took a special interest in me. It happened a long time ago, and yet it's kind of funny. I don't even remember her name, but what a difference she made in my life."

Harold possessed the rare gift of effective communication. A natural story teller, he often used real life accounts of great people, past or present, to illustrate his sermons. One of his favorite illustrations was the story of a frustrated Sunday School teacher named Edward Kimball.

One day Mr. Kimball went to the shoe store where Dwight L. Moody was working, wrapping shoes. He put his hand on Mr. Moody's shoulder and talked briefly of Jesus' love for him. That was all. It has been said that up until that moment, D. L. Moody had not known that he possessed a soul. "Moody lingered many times over that sweet moment. Many times in future years he relived that strange ecstasy of a young man who had just become a new creature in Christ Jesus." With stories of such impact, Harold was able to hold his audience in rapt attention.

TEACHING HIS FIRST CLASS

In February, 1933, at age 20, Harold was asked to teach the intermediate department of the Sunday School at Angelus Temple. He compiled a series of lectures dealing with Science and the Bible, which touched on astronomy, botany, biology, anthropology, physiology and meteorology.

He used pictorial illustrations with permission from the University of Southern California's Department of Visual

Education. They were a tremendous success. God used this effective method to teach impressionable minds in an impressive way. These lectures were presented all over the United States, Australia and many other places around the world.

PEOPLE WHO MADE A DIFFERENCE

The impressionable life of young Harold Chalfant was shaped by strong, spiritual leadership. Harold was touched by those who reflected the radiant energy of the Holy Spirit in their own lives.

It's inspiring to consider some of the individuals who made a definite impact on his life. Each of these individuals is a vivid example of the simple, yet profound truth that would characterize the Chalfant ministry; life touching life.

- His Mother, Nora Doyle Chalfant, who secretly and overtly molded his life by her Godly influence and daily prayer.

- Aimee Semple McPherson, who led him to Christ. Her courageous spirit inspired him to follow in the footsteps of Jesus.

- Dr. A. P. Gouthey, whose scholarly, spiritual character left an indelible mark upon his heart and mind.

- Dr. Sidney Correll, who was the first to enlighten his mind with thrilling missionary messages. He caused Harold to think of a lost world without Christ as a personal responsibility.

- Rev. Hubert Mitchell, founder and director of Los Angeles Youth for Christ. Rev. Mitchell also serves as director of Inter–Church Go Ye Fellowship. He founded the Televisitation ministry in 1963. For many years he served as a missionary to India and

Indonesia. The Mitchell family influenced Harold from school days.

- Dr. Watson B. Teaford, former Dean of L.I.F.E. College and former pastor of Angelus Temple. Ingenious and wise in counsel, Dr. Teaford specialized in teaching Bible doctrine, implementing in Harold a desire, "*To study to show himself approved unto God, a workman that needeth not to be ashamed.*" (II Timothy 2:15)

- Dr. Clarence Hall, was Angelus Temple's first Crusader Youth President. As a youth motivator, he inspired consecrated leadership in Harold and opened the door to youth ministry not only in Angelus Temple but subsequently around the world.

I Took A Piece Of Plastic Clay

I took a piece of plastic clay
And idly fashioned it one day,
And as my fingers pressed it still,
It moved and yielded at my will.
I came again when days were passed
The bit of clay was hard at last.
The form I gave it, still it bore,
But I could change that form no more.
I took a piece of living clay
And gently formed it day by day
And molded with my powers and art,
A young child's soft and yielding heart.
I came again when years were gone,
It was a man, I looked upon
He still that early impress wore,
But I could change him never more.
Author Unknown

Mr. Chalfant quoted this poem at public forums, conferences, organizations and mass church services.

Chapter 5
Ministering To Youth

In July 1935, at the age of 20, Harold Chalfant was appointed the International Crusader Commander by the late Aimee Semple McPherson. The appointment entailed directing all youth activities of the Foursquare Denomination. This responsibility was a perfect métier for an individual with both the kinetic temperament and passion to reach youth that Harold possessed.

Young Chalfant was convinced that Christian Summer Camps would be the most effective tool for realizing his evangelistic vision. His strong desire to see this project get off the ground was like a mandate from God. It seemed that each practical step along the way had been explicitly communicated to him by the Holy Spirit.

To proceed, he needed authorization from the corporate leaders to initiate the camping program. Standing before those of such authority and stature, he may have felt a little like the Apostle Paul on the day he made his defense before King Agrippa. Random thoughts darted through his mind...

"What if I'm rejected?"

"What if they think I'm some kind of a nut?" (a favorite expression)

"What if...?"

The reckless side of his nature won out over the negatives. Although he devoted considerable thought to the seriousness of this meeting, he came to the conclusion that the needs of the young people could not be put on the back–burner.

As he sat in the office of Harriet Jordan, Vice President of the corporation, he promptly got to the point by asking permission to start a summer camp for youth in the mountains. Miss Jordan didn't have the faintest idea what he was talking about. Her concept of a camp was temporary in nature, finding a public facility somewhere in the mountains, then holding a series of revival meetings, similar to the old–fashioned brush arbor services so popular in the past. This was NOT Harold's concept of youth camps. In the ensuing moments, he had the opportunity to present his ideas to a very open–minded woman who turned out to be very receptive to his mission.

"You know, Miss Jordan," he said as he pursed his lips firmly, then riveted his intense dark eyes on her face, "the burden of my heart is to organize Christian Summer Camps. Our kids get kicked around 365 days a year. I believe it's time we get them into the mountains for a spiritual retreat, for a time of soul searching where they can examine their lives and draw near to God."

Even at the age of 20, he recognized the moral and spiritual dilemma of our time. He had witnessed gang life in the schools and on the streets. He had seen broken, dysfunctional families, characterized by physical abuse, substance abuse, incest, rape, killings and loathsome disease. This kind of environment was producing more and more children with severe emotional and mental problems.

Harold believed in saving the boys and girls now, rather than trying to salvage their lives later, when it was often too late. Getting them away from an unwholesome environment, if only for a week, could hopefully be the turning point in their lives.

Miss Jordan listened with avid interest as he laid bare the burden of his soul. With inspired enthusiasm he spoke of the availability of camp grounds which could be leased from the City of Los Angeles for one, or two or three weeks at a time for the retreats.

Carefully, he explained a format for daily activities. There would be a bugle call to begin the day, a time of morning Bible study, organized sports in the afternoon, as well as many other kinds of planned recreation. In the early evening, Victory Circle would be held around a glowing camp fire. Campers would participate in a time of inspirational singing, followed by an evangelistic service in the main auditorium. In the middle of the week, there would be a fun night featuring skits and music. All through the week exciting events would take place.

After Harold's impassioned speech, Miss Jordan was convinced that his ideas were good. Permission was granted. It was a historical moment. The future would disclose the far–reaching results of that meeting.

CHAPTER 6
SUMMER CAMP PROGRAM

The plans to initiate a summer camping program took place in the spring of 1934. Officials and youth representatives met regularly at Clifton's Cafeteria in downtown Los Angeles. Many favored Pacific Palisades Conference Center, but Harold Chalfant was personally convinced that camps should be conducted in the mountains.

During his emotional talk on a campsite he quoted a poem written by his wise and trusted mentor Dr. A. P. Gouthey, "Give Me The Deep And Solemn Woods." After that it was unanimously voted to have the first camp at Seeley, which is not far from Crestline.

Give Me The Deep Solemn Woods

Give me the deep solemn woods
Where never a sound is heard
Save the rustle of a falling leaf
Or the twitter of a bird.
My Palace built by God's own hand
Pillared and roofed with green,
Bedecked with blossoms rare and fresh
And hung with woodbine screen.
My music is the minstrel wind

23

That harps on sturdy pines,
And stirs the heart to deepest depths
Like distant tower chimes.
My Cathedral is the mountains high
I worship at its shrine,
For altar fire the Sunset's flame
That burns like light divine.
Here the Infinite seems most real
I feel His presence near,
and when the daylight slowly dies
My heart can know no fear.
And when life's sunset fills my days
With shadows soft and deep,
I'd be laid here beneath the pines
Where stars their vigil keep.
                    Dr. A. P. Gouthey

Camp Seeley, owned by the Playground and Recreation Department of the City of Los Angeles, granted the organization its first contract to operate a youth camp in 1934. Watson B. Teaford directed the camp the first year. Since Harold was only 20, he was too young to sign the lease, but Dr. Teaford was there to sign for him. That first year there were 85 campers enrolled.

Roy Bell Volunteers

There was a bright young man from the Ventura church named Roy Bell who became a motivator to challenge the young people from his group to go to camp. He showed exceptional talent in organization and was instrumental in bringing nearly half the campers to Camp Seeley. As the Lord persistently nudged him to do volunteer work in the camps, he became Harold's loyal right hand man, serving as camp controller. One of his many assignments was surveying land for purchase.

As the Great Depression deepened Harold found that he did not have enough money to reserve a place at camp. But that didn't stop him. He and his buddy, Lee Athens, camped out on the mountain side every night with sleeping bags, then in the morning Harold would go down the hill to direct camp.

Harold's leadership style was dynamic, orderly and well–organized. His commitment to running a tight ship produced a pattern of administration that brought honor and glory to Jesus Christ.

A number of the campers were 10–15 years older than Harold, so it was imperative that he conduct himself with the maturity befitting a leader. Otherwise, there might have been an outbreak of riot instead of revival. As Harold would put it, "No way!"

GROWING PAINS

The second year 150 campers enrolled at Camp Radford. That same year, 1935, camps opened in the Northwest District (covering Oregon, Washington and Canada) at Tressle Glen Camp. At Radford they doubled numerically each year – 150, 300, 600. Since Camp Radford could accommodate only 425 at a time, the next step was to divide into two sessions. Some 19,000 boys and girls passed through its portals during the Radford days.

In those early depression days, one person could enroll for a dollar a day, eight dollars a week, including room and board. The biggest problem was getting the finances together to go to camp.

Harold's vision for camping expanded into the eastern part of the country. The first camp opened in Muskegon, Michigan. Through the years the number of camps continued to escalate.

By 1936, the first camp outside the United States was started in Central America. At that time 17 year old Leland Edwards, son of Dr. A. F. Edwards, missionary to Panama, came home on furlough to attend Camp Radford in California. Leland returned to Panama with renewed enthusiasm to start camps.

CHAPTER 7
VICTORY CIRCLE

Synonymous with summer camps is Victory Circle. Every night at twilight campers would assemble in an outdoor amphitheater. A fire pit glowed with smoldering embers ready to ignite into a blazing fire. The atmosphere was charged with a source of spiritual expectation conducive to worship, praise and challenge. The outdoor cathedral was uniquely picturesque, with lofty pines, firs and fragrant cedar trees dominating the mountainous landscape.

A myriad of stars decorated the vast domain of heaven with their luminous light. It was easy to discern a quickening of Spirit as Psalm 19:1 comes to mind...

"The heavens are telling the glory of God: they are a marvelous display of his craftsmanship. Day and night they keep telling about God. Without a sound or word, silent in the skies, their message reaches out to all the world."

The song leader would open with prayer, then the young audience of over 400 campers was led in a series of inspirational songs, beautiful in theme, with the flowing movement of Word and testimony.

"Turn Your Eyes Upon Jesus" is a chorus remembered so well. Another one that has been an all–time favorite:

> "Standing somewhere in the shadows, You'll find Jesus.
> He's the One who always cares and understands...
> Standing somewhere in the shadows you will find Him,
> And you'll know Him by the nail prints in His hand."

Campers were encouraged and given an opportunity to seek God through the medium of prayer. Through petition they would express their inner needs: their conflicts and conquests, their struggles, temptations and triumphs, their sorrows and joys, their failure and victories.

It was a sharing time. It was a caring time. It was a time to meet God and discover that there is hope in Jesus Christ.

Something spontaneous and electric would happen. Suddenly the stranger who sat next to you did not seem like a stranger anymore. Hands were clasped in a spirit of worship and praise toward God. The Holy Spirit was melting and bonding in unity a body of believers who wanted nothing more than to be used of God. They became strangely aware, for the first time, that God wanted living sacrifices, not dead ones. They felt an incredible closeness to God, and the desire for active service welled up within them.

Victory Circle was held every night of the week, under the stars. On the last night of camp the Commitment Service was held with the same format as Victory Circle. The only difference was that each person was given a pine cone, representing his life, to be thrown into the fire at the conclusion of the service as an act of consecration.

After worship, the speaker walked toward the open fire pit, which was built around a low retaining wall. He stepped upon the improvised platform to speak. His name was Harold Chalfant.

The first impression of Harold was vivid. He was tall, slender and under the age of twenty–five. He was dressed in field fatigues, resembling that of an outdoorsman or an explorer. His commanding presence elicited respect and rapt attention. The flames created a silhouette against the backdrop of the pale moonlight.

The sound of Harold's words vibrated like lightning, thunder and fire. A captive audience was fascinated by his personal magnetism. One must keep in mind the campers were between 14 to 18 years of age, so they were young, impressionable, and easily influenced in their eagerness to follow a role model of heroic stature.

After Harold's message, an appealing invitation challenged the young people to move forward toward the fire pit, expressing an act of dedication. At the propitious moment, each boy and girl would throw a pine cone into the roaring fire, symbolic of the ministry of the Holy Spirit burning out the dross, cleansing, healing and setting on fire each believing heart which is really serious before God.

Out of the flame came lives surrendered as a living sacrifice to be used by the Lord, whenever and wherever He chose. It was an unforgettable scene that has been repeated many thousands of times over. God used a Victory Circle and a Commitment Service to motivate armies of youth into active Christian service.

1942 FIRE OUTBREAK AT CAMP RADFORD

During the summer of '42, summer camp had been in full swing for three weeks. War time food rationing was in effect. To provide for 1500 campers was quite a challenge.

On one particular Tuesday morning, Roy Bell (also known as "Pops") and his wife Gladys, had gone down the hill to purchase supplies for the new week. Returning back to camp in their truck loaded with supplies, they saw ominous billows of black smoke inundating the mountain ahead of them. The forest rangers stopped them and told them of a plane crash in the mountains. Fire had then erupted sweeping up the river canyon.

The fire fighters recruited about 100 young men from the camp to deal with the emergency. The rest of the camp population was evacuated to a safe area. "Pops" Bell, along with others, formed a caravan, shuttling 500 campers back and forth to Barton Flats, where they stayed the night making the best of a dangerous and unpleasant situation.

During the evacuation Harold was busy creating a fire break. Using a massive bull dozer, he scooped up tons of brush and flammable debris, forming a clear strip of land around the camp grounds. As a result, Harold's efforts were successful, as the fire spread only as far as a wire fence enclosure which extended up the hill to the Radford grounds.

Miraculously, both the camp and many lives were saved.

CHAPTER 8
WINDS OF CHANGE

The winds of change brought about an explosion of growth in the Southern California District, which prompted immediate action in locating a suitable denominationally owned camping ground. Many summit meetings were held to discuss plans and hopes for the future. Most of the sessions were again held at Clifton's cafeteria. For a period of months Harold along with his staff (comprised of Dr. and Mrs. Earl Dorrance, Roy Bell, Don Stauffer and Dick Silvius) drove all over the San Bernardino Mountains, looking for property. At last a location was found upon which Camp Cedar Crest stands today. The deed records that on April 17, 1946, Camp Cedar Crest was purchased.

On May 30, 1946 a huge barbecue was held on the site. Leaders walked all over the hillsides dedicating the property and selecting locations for future buildings. The buildings already on the property included the Bemis home which became the first Candy Store and the Infirmary, which burned to the ground in 1956. The new infirmary was built in 1958. During the interim, the center of the Orange Belt Cabin was used as the infirmary.

During the four and a half years in which Camp Cedar Crest was being built, the youth camps continued to utilize the Camp Radford grounds. The 85 acres of prime property was purchased for $18,000. Today the land is valued at over $2,000,000 dollars. The remaining undeveloped 45 acres of land is worth approximately $2,000,000 dollars.

On some Fridays and Saturdays nearly 250 unpaid workers would be busy on site. It was common to see skilled laborers like tile setters, cement men, electrical contractors, roofers and plasterers using their weekends to serve God, and with great results. When it came time to plaster the dining room, 35 volunteers came up to help and completed the project in one day.

The virgin territory had to be explored and developed for use. One summer Harold worked three and a half months with a bulldozer, literally moving mountains of dirt to make the ball diamond. He shoveled tons of old red cedar that had been in a forest fire over 100 years ago. Some of the giant cedars are still there. That's how Cedar Crest got its name.

In building Cedar Crest, lumber was difficult to get; so Harold and his crew tore down all the bridges, by contract, on the narrow gauge railroads between Santa Barbara and San Luis Obispo. So the timber at Cedar Crest came from those railroad bridges.

One of the huge beams "kicked out" and broke Harold's back in two places. So when he talked of everything having a special meaning for him, it did, in this instance. He saved one chunk of cedar, put it on a truck, then took it to the mill and had it sliced and planed for the mantle in his home. The left over wood he made into a clock over the mantle.

As a result of these efforts, there are now 229 Foursquare camps situated throughout 16 nations of the world. And to think it all started in 1933 with Harold Chalfant and 85 kids at Camp Seeley! The camps in Southern California were divided into districts including the Coastal, Mountain, Valley and Desert Divisions. Camps were held all summer, with a different group coming in every Saturday. To accommodate 500 campers per week required much planning and organization.

Another amazing aspect of God's work at Camp Cedar Crest is that over 16 different organizations have used the camp. By actual count, some 300,000 boys and girls have attended Camp Cedar Crest. For over four and a half years, great efforts were made at fundraising and recruiting volunteer labor with much success.

YOUTH RALLIES

The camps, created the inspiration for youth rallies. During the summer camps there had been wonderful opportunities for fellowship among the youth of the church. Young people from Santa Barbara to San Diego, from Angelus Temple to Yuma, Arizona made friends and encouraged each other in the Lord. To continue these opportunities for growth, fall and winter rallies were started each month in the Divisions. They were so successful that trains were leased to bring young people together en masse. So great was the excitement that youth groups from San Diego would think nothing of making a 12 hour round trip to join with other fellowships in Santa Barbara. These gatherings soon developed into huge youth rallies. At the Shrine Auditorium, 8,000 were turned away. To accommodate the demand, these gatherings moved to the Hollywood Bowl.

The Santa Barbara Train Rally was a historical first in the Crusader youth movement of the Foursquare denomination. Harold, with the able assistance of Roy Bell, shared the vision of this rally with youth from all over the Southland. In strategic positions outstanding leaders such as Don Stauffer from the Mountain Division, Earle Williams from the Valley

Division, Clifford Musgrove from the Central Division and Leita Mae Steward from the Desert Division assisted in making the Santa Barbara Train Rally a reality.

DEPRESSION DAYS.

Envision the year 1939... Families were having a tough time making ends meet. There was no work, no money, and little food. Thousands were homeless, living on the streets. For young people, especially, it seemed a hopeless situation.

World dictators in the personages of Adolf Hitler and Benito Mussolini were rising to power. War clouds were gathering as World War II loomed upon the horizon. Our young men were leaving for the military and everything seemed uncertain and frightening.

All that time, young people were hungry for strong leadership and a real and lasting cause to believe in. At the Santa Barbara rally, many found the purpose and meaning they longed for in the person of Jesus Christ.

The Train Rally was dramatic. Witnesses saw 5,000 young people converge upon the city of Santa Barbara, inundating the area with dozens of marching bands, colorfully decorated horses and bright patriotic flags waving in the air. Aimee Semple McPherson led the parade, riding in a Packard convertible. Throngs of expectant people lined the streets to watch the procession.

The young people marched 5,000 strong all the way to the Santa Barbara Bowl to participate in a tremendous youth rally. Imagine a huge group of excited young people, gathered together with no threat of violence, no substance abuse, or destructive intentions. There on the streets of Santa Barbara was a remnant of the church of God, marching as a mighty army exalting the Lord Jesus Christ as King of Kings and Lord of Lords!

"Talk about a high," said Earle Williams. "There's never been anything like it before, or since." It had an overwhelming spiritual impact that momentous day.

A Mother's Prayer

God, Father of Freedom, look after that boy of mine, wherever he may be. Walk in upon him. Talk with him during the silent watches of the night, and spur him to bravery when he faces the cruel foe. Transfer my prayer to his heart.

Keep my boy inspired by the never–dying faith in his God. Throughout all the long days of a hopeful victory, wherever his duty takes him, keep his spirit high and his purpose unwavering. Make him a loyal friend. Nourish him with the love that I gave him at birth, and satisfy the hunger of his soul with the knowledge of my prayer. He is my choicest treasure.

Take care of him, God. Keep him in health and sustain him under every possible circumstance. I once warmed him under my heart. You warm him anew in his shelter under the stars. Touch him with my smile of cheer and comfort, and my full confidence in his every brave pursuit.

Fail him not — and may he not fail You, his country, nor the mother who bore him.

Author Unknown

Mr. Chalfant quoted this prayer during W.W.II when so many of the men were away serving our country.

Harold at 18 years old

George and Nora Chalfant

Harold & his Mother, Nora

Former Angelus Temple youth leaders from left to right: W.B. Teaford, Hubert Mitchell, George Johnson, Clarence Hall, Harold Chalfant, Luther Meier, Roy Bell, Earle Williams, Charles Meir, Loren Grant.

Harold (Van Cleave) Chalfant plans a saxaphone solo at camp reunion

Sister Aimee at Santa Barbara Crusade Rally

Aimee Semple McPherson

Harold at the Shrine Auditorium youth rally

Harold presents trophy to Don Stauffer at Radford Reunion

A. P. Gouthey

Don Stauffer

Loren Grant

Dr. Clair Britton

Dean Miller with
President Eisenhower

Angelus Temple

Inside Angelus Temple

Angelus Temple Glee Club with Audrey Meier

Angelus Temple Crusaders 1941

Santa Barbara Train Rally

Inside of Coach

Angelus Temple Silver Band

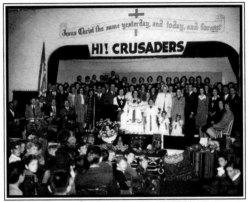

District Crusader Rally

Sister Aimee leads the parade at
Santa Barbara

Hollywood Bowl Rally

Harold emcees at the Hollywood Bowl

Harold leads songs at Angelus Temple Rally

Harold plans an international
convention

Shrine Auditorium Rally

Platform Scene at the Shrine Auditorium Rally

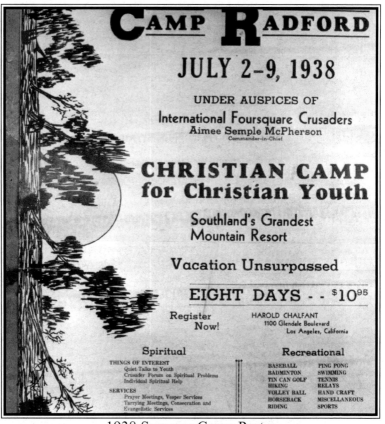

1938 Summer Camp Poster

Camp Radford Mess Hall

Radford Baseball Field

Camp Radford Swimming Pool

First Camp at Radford

Mountain

Valley

Coastal

Division 1946

Division 1946

Division 1947

Radford Scenic View

Radford Scenic View

Winter at Radford

Winter Scene

Construction at Cedar Crest

Little George strikes out

Ulphin Davis and Harold

Homer & Jethro

Baking a cake

International Youth Leaders left to right: **Front row** Joy
Larson, Elsie Chalfant, Isabelle Helmle, Maxine Talbot,
Helen Jensen, Carolyn Siesser, Emma Davis, Hope Vollmer
and Cappy Gwillim. **Back Row** Art Larson, Harold
Chalfant, Max Siesser, Paul Talbot, Jerry Jensen, Ulphin
Davis and Jack Gwillim.

Chapter 9
Leaders Who Made
A Difference

"For God's sake give me the young man who has brains enough
to make a fool of himself."

R. L. Stevenson

Harold Chalfant dared to become "a fool for Christ's sake."
In the early 1930s, God used Harold as a catalyst for change
in founding youth camps, under the auspices of the
International Church of the Foursquare Gospel. His aggres-
sive and inspired leadership ignited a flame of hope among
other denominations of that era. They benefited from his
methods of approach by modeling their own summer youth
camps after his vision of reaching youth for Christ. It was a
renaissance of life with a purpose for youth across the land.
The tangible results are evidenced today.

Harold also championed the cause of world–wide missions
in our time. The genius of his life was that he was "sold out"
to the express will of God. His legendary leadership challenged hundreds of thousands of young people. In unprece-
dented numbers they scattered to the ends of the earth, reaching a lost world for Christ.

During an informal interview, just before his passing, Harold was asked to name some of the leaders who came out of the camping program. The list is unending, but in that extemporaneous, impromptu moment he mentioned a few of the men and women still of note in the Body of Christ today.

- Dean Miller founded and pastored the Presbyterian Church in Palm Desert, California. He was President Dwight D. Eisenhower's Pastor. Dean officiated at President Eisenhower's funeral service. As Harold remembered him, "Dean was a boy who came out of the old Echo Park gang. He grew up on the streets of Echo Park and Sunset Boulevard."

- Of Earle Williams he said, "An inspired leader among youth. Earle pioneered Gospel Recording and today is very active in the International Bible Institute, which he founded."

- Of Roy McKeown: "A visionary and a compassionate man. Roy lived in my home as a young student in Bible College. Today Roy is founder and president of World Opportunities International. His Global Outreach Ministry strongly assists those in need. His work with Third World Countries knows no boundaries."

- Of Carl Cadonau: "Carl is owner of the Alpenrose Dairy, Portland, Oregon. It is the largest dairy in the Northwest, but also serves as a tourist attraction like Knotts Berry Farm. Carl and his sister, Anita Cadonau Birkland, were young people who came out of the Trestle Glen Crusader Camp in Oregon."

- Of Guy Martin: "He was greatly used of God as a great influence and inspiration during the days at

Camp Radford. For years he has been a very successful automobile distributor in Southern California. Guy serves on the board of the Billy Graham Evangelistic Association."

- Of Don Stauffer: "Don started going to camps at 13 years of age. He ran all the youth activities at Camp Radford and Cedar Crest. Don is one of the finest professional commercial photographers in the United States. He was the official photographer for the Rams professional football team. He was a tremendous asset to the youth program."

- Of Ulphin and Emma Davis: "They were the Directors of Youth and Christian Education in the Northwest for many years. I thought Ulphin was a God–made comedian. The young people loved him. On Skit Night he was a sensation. When some Hollywood producers saw a film clip of Ulphin doing his famous ABC Sermon, they wanted to sign him immediately for a TV slot on one of the major networks. This Christian man was blessed with the gift of humor. He made people laugh, all for glory to God."

- And finally: "Pastor Charles 'Chuck' Smith is a man whom God is using to touch virtually hundreds of thousands of lives today. He was a boy whose life was literally turned around while attending Crusader Camps. Chuck's life has been singularly blessed with the anointing of the Holy Spirit of God upon it. I spoke at Chuck's church a few years back to 24,000 young people. What a thrill."

This list of people touched by the commitment and dedication of Harold Chalfant is extensive. Literally thousands of other stories could be told of lives changed and hearts set afire for Jesus Christ as a result of the summer camping program and youth rallies.

Obedience

I said, "Let me walk in the field."
He said, "No; walk in the town."
I said, "There are no flowers there."
He said, "No flowers, but a crown."
I said, "But the skies are black,
There is nothing but noise and din."
And He wept as He sent me back.
"There is more," He said; "There is sin."
I said, "But the air is thick
And fogs are veiling the sun."
He answered, "Yet souls are sick,
And souls in the dark undone."
I said, "I shall miss the light,
And friends will miss me, they say."
He answered, "Choose tonight
If I am to miss you, or they."
I pleaded for time to be given.
He said, "Is it hard to decide?
It will not seem hard in Heaven
To have followed the steps of your Guide.
I cast one look at the fields
Then set my face to the town;
He said, "My child, do you yield?
Will you leave the flowers for the crown?"
Then into His hand went mine;
And into my heart came He;
And I walk in a light divine,
The path I had feared to see.

George MacDonald

PART II
A MINISTRY TO THE WORLD

CHAPTER 10
A HEART FOR THE WORLD

At age 22, Harold was chosen to serve as a member of the Foursquare Missionary Cabinet, a position he held for 27 years. In 1938, he made his first overseas trip to South and Central America. This was the beginning of one of the greatest missionary quests of our time.

Harold believed unequivocally in the Biblical statement, *"For the Son of man is come to SEEK and to SAVE that which was lost."* (Luke 19:10) There was little room for doubt that God's priority for His people was bringing His truth to those who have never heard.

Harold, with his wife Elsie, left from San Pedro harbor on the Panama Pacific line. They sailed on the S.S. Pennsylvania, which at that time was the largest ship that went from Los Angeles to New York, through the Panama Canal.

The night they embarked from San Pedro, Loren Grant, Director of the Angelus Temple Choir, came down with a tremendous group of glee club singers. They saw the Chalfants off with several songs in keeping with the nautical setting, such as "Harbor lights," and "Sail On, Sail On." It was a tender, impressive moment, and one they would always remember.

The next morning Harold was talking to a German passenger aboard ship who asked him, "Who were those people singing to last night?" Harold let the man talk for a few moments without saying much; but finally, as the man said, "By God, that was the most beautiful singing I ever heard." Harold, somewhat embarrassed, shyly remarked, "They were singing to us."

The Chalfants spent the next three weeks visiting the twenty–four mission stations in the interior of Panama. Harold inherited quite a substantial spiritual legacy in Panama.

Many times during Harold's missionary messages he gave the dramatic account of the call of Dr. A. F. Edwards to the Central American country. It was a moving, impelling story that inspired hope in times when doubt and confusion concerning the supernatural acts of God were so common. No one could hear this talk without being confronted with the truth God still speaks, directs and leads His children in the affairs of their lives today.

Dr. A. F. Edwards was a graduate of L.I.F.E. Bible College in 1926. After graduation, he prayerfully sought the Lord for divine direction in his life. While praying at Angelus Temple, God gave him a vivid and vitalizing vision of service in the foreign field. The manifestation lasted for several hours.

While praying in the spirit, God revealed to him a bearded man of white hair, weeping continuously with great anguish of soul. All around this elderly man were multitudes of souls, perishing without a saving knowledge of Jesus Christ.

It was as though the entire country of Panama flashed before his eyes. As he remained in the vision, the travail for souls became heavier, until at last he heard the call: "Will You Go?" On bended knee and with intense agony of spirit, he said, "Yes Lord, I will go. I will give my heart and life to Panama." With the vision ever before him, Dr. and Mrs. Edwards went to Panama. There he saw this mission field as he had seen it through the eye of faith so many years before.

God blessed his faithful efforts. After nine years of labor on the Panamanian field, he had opened twenty–four mission stations (1935).

A number of years later, Dr. Edwards heard of an old missionary who was very ill and dying in the Gorgas Hospital in the Canal Zone. He went to the hospital to visit him. As he stepped into the hospital ward, it seemed as though the room was filled with the radiant presence of God.

There, lying on a hospital cot was an old man with a great, flowing beard. Was it a dream? An illusion? It seemed unreal. There before him lay the white haired old gentleman he had seen so many years before in his vision. The old man's name was Rev. Latham, a missionary from the Cumberland Presbyterian Church. It is supposed that he was the first Protestant missionary to go to the Republic of Panama.

When Rev. Latham saw Dr. Edwards, his face glowed with joy in the Holy Spirit. After speaking with the gift of tongues, he whispered faintly, "You are the man whom God has called to finish the work I have started in Central America." Rev. Latham took the hand of Dr. Edwards and held it – so happy the Lord had heard his prayer – and so happy Dr. Edwards had arrived in time to receive his last words of blessing. This beautiful encounter confirmed God's approval and guidance upon Dr. Edwards life.

Dr. Edwards was visibly moved with emotion. Tears began to run down his cheeks, for here before him was the man he had seen in his vision so many years before – the man who had given fifty years of his life toiling in service on the foreign field.

Harold had in his possession a musty diary that had belonged to Rev. Latham. In his diary he told how fanatics stoned him in the interior. Several times he was left unconscious to die, but the Lord sustained him.

Harold had the opportunity of walking through the old dilapidated mission that had fallen apart. The walls were down and the floors were eaten by white ants. As he walked in the midst of the ruins, the splendor and glory of the Lord swept over him as he realized with joy the privilege of being able to carry on the great work of that godly missionary.

On one occasion, Harold openly remarked how much he loved the Panamanian children, and when he awakened early the next morning, he heard little ones crying. Much to his astonishment, he discovered six little infants had been placed under his hammock! Right then he decided that in the future, he would have to be more careful in expressing his love for those lovable Panamanian babies.

PRICELESS LEGACY

Evident in the economy of divine providence, God had simultaneously dove–tailed His plan and purpose through the human agency of Rev. Latham (the white haired missionary, with the flowing beard), who laid the foundation for the work, then spoke to the heart of Dr. A. F. Edwards in the United States by giving him a vision and a stirring call to the field, to carry on with the great work in Panama. The legacy of "not being disobedient unto the heavenly vision", (Acts 26:19) had been passed down three generations to Harold Chalfant.

CHAPTER 11
GREEN HELL OF BOLIVIA

After leaving Panama, Harold traveled without Elsie down the coast of South America, visiting Colombia, Ecuador and Peru. After disembarking at Mollendo, Peru he boarded a train that followed the highest railroad in the world, 15,500 feet. He crossed Lake Titicaca and then made connections to fly over the jungles to Trinidad, Bolivia, the capital of the Beni Province.

Bolivia lies in the very heart of South America with no outlet to the ocean, so it is very difficult to get into and out of that country. Had he not gone by plane, he would have had to travel by river boat and pack train to Trinidad, a journey which would have taken nearly six weeks to complete.

In Trinidad, Bolivia, Harold found a very progressive missions work under the able ministry of the Anderson family. They had obtained the largest building in Trinidad for services, yet it was still inadequate to accommodate the crowds. They were building a new church, which when completed, would be one of the finest buildings in Trinidad. Harold stayed ten days in the city preaching every night, through an interpreter, to the Bolivians. The people were a joy and a delight to him.

When Jack Anderson (a 19 year old Crusader Missionary) returned from a Sironois Indian village, he offered to act as Harold's guide and take him back through the dangerous swamps and jungles to camp. The village was some fifty miles through the jungle, but we in the United States cannot fully realize the challenges those fifty miles would involve.

There are twelve crocodile, alligator and boa–infested swamps to cross, some three miles wide and fifteen miles long. One of the most dangerous swamps in all Bolivia is between Trinidad and the Indian village. It is so dangerous that no Bolivian had ever crossed it.

The government men go around the swamp–infested jungle when they have official business with the Andersons. Jack and his brother Paul, however, cross the swamp two and three times a week. Their express purpose is to reach the Sironois people with the life–changing power of the Lord Jesus Christ.

The swamps were not the only source of danger that Harold and the Andersons had to cope with. Even the most innocent, lowly example of local wildlife can turn out to be extremely dangerous.

On one trip through the jungle, Harold started to pick up a caterpillar. Jack yelled, "Don't touch that!"

"Why?"

"This is one of the most poisonous insects we have in the jungle," he said. "If it bites you, you will become paralyzed."

"Have you ever been bitten?", Harold asked.

"Twice." The first time the left side of my body was paralyzed. I was in such agony I rolled on the ground and began crying for the Lord to let me die."

One night along the trail Jack and Harold stopped at an old Indian's place. They had been in the saddle twelve hours. They literally fell off their horses, exhausted. Harold took off his boots and emptied the water out of them, then took off his socks and squeezed the water out of them – then did the same thing with his trousers and shirt.

The boys made their beds by taking their old saddle blankets and throwing them on the ground.

Harold described the episode, "Sometimes the horses have great running sores on their backs, perhaps six inches wide. You can look right down to the spine. They sometimes became so exhausted going through the swamps that we had to beat them until their sides were bleeding. We had to do it to get them to go on lest they die in the swamp.

"Many times they could not, so we would let them rest for a few hours, then pray and ask God to give them strength to get us through the swamps. We dared not stop in the swamps as it meant our lives.

"Making our beds was something else. We took the dirty, bloody, and puss soaked saddle blankets, put a rubber poncho on top of them, placed mosquito netting as thick as muslin on it – then crawled inside.

"You get used to it and come to like the suffocating smell because it is so much better than the infectious blood suckers that get into your bed, plus the little insects called 'neewa' which get into your body, blood, flesh, hair and almost drive you crazy. Ticks the size of a man's finger would get into your bed at night if it weren't for the mosquito net. Blood suckers are one thing, but there were also snakes and bats.

"In the water there is a great yellow snake about nine or ten feet long which can lash you on the side of your body, causing great sores. The Boa Constrictors are often twenty five to thirty feet in length. They are capable of swallowing a thousand to fifteen hundred pound steer by crushing the life out of it. There is not a bone left that has not been broken. After the boa stretches out to a length of about fifteen feet, it swallows the steer."

Jack and Paul found Boas with the steer inside except for the head and horns which cannot be swallowed. The horns and head must lie on the ground until the head decomposes which takes perhaps a month or two. These great snakes would not have to crush a man to swallow him.

The gracious old Indian cooked a meal for Harold and Jack that night. Having just butchered a cow, he roasted the meat in ashes, and baked the yucca root for bread. Famished from hunger, they ate every bit of it, not giving a second thought to the gaping running sore (Leprosy or Cancer) on the old Indian's chest.

With the meal they were served some native tea, stored in a can. No coffee for Harold. Harold stirred it up and thought it was quite good, except for what he thought were tea leaves.

The next morning when breakfast was served, Harold asked, "Where are the leaves in the tea?"
Jack answered, "There aren't any leaves in the tea."
"Then what was in my tea last night?" Harold responded.
"Look in the sugar." Jack prompted.

The brown sugar was literally black with the heads and bodies of ants, wasps and bees. Jack wouldn't tell him anything. He just let him "live and learn" as they went along.

"Take your spoon," Jack said, "Throw in some sugar, stir it up until the sugar dissolves. In a few moments all the heads, bodies, legs and wings will float to the top."

Harold yelled, "Then what?"

You have three options," declared Jack. You can drink it by straining it through your teeth, you can scoop them out, or you can blow the whole bunch off at one time!"

One Night in an Ox Cart

Jack had come down with pneumonia. It had taken them seven days to go twenty five miles. As the sun was setting, they were standing in the middle of a great swamp, many days from home. The bull alligators were bellowing all around them. Jack was dying; he had slipped off into unconsciousness. Paul knelt beside him and began talking to God...

"Lord," he said. "If Jack lives it will only be by mercy. If Jack dies, everything here dies. This work dies. Now Lord, you take care of the boy."

Paul watched with vigilance all through the night. Jack's lungs had collapsed, full of poison. After a couple of hours, Paul prayed again. As he watched Jack, he noticed his eyes begin to flutter. Soon Jack sat up smiling. He was healed, the infection gone! God had wrought a miracle. Jack and Paul resumed their trip and started back to the savage camp.

Harold Spoke of the Demon Powers...

"It is not the tigers, jaguars, lions, poisonous snakes or the ravages of disease that get under the hide of a man; the flies that bite and hatch a worm as long as your finger, which crawls under the skin; the stomach worms eighteen inches long, that take the life out of a person. There are a thousand and one things, to be sure, that might discourage and defeat the missionary. But the demon power which is manifested on every side is the worst nightmare of all..."

Evil Entity Encounter

On one occasion, after Jack had gone to bed, there in the moonlight during the middle of the night, Jack saw a stranger. He walked up behind the stranger and started quietly to lay his hand on his shoulder, but the stranger suddenly disappeared. It was a demon. Jack had been alone in the jungle for three months. Harold asked Jack, "What did you do?" Jack answered, "That one time I was so scared I fell on the ground and lay there trembling and crying the rest of the night.

"When we come face to face with the demons, we just say, *'Greater is He that is in you than he that is in the world.'*" (I John 4:4) They stand on the scripture.

"Sometimes," Jack said, "The demons will come into the savage huts and try to snatch the babies from their mother's arms." Jack and Paul would go out to the huts and demand that the demons flee in the name of Jesus!

In speaking of the work in Bolivia, Harold continued to say, "The most precious thing about the boys' work is how tirelessly they have labored clearing off the seven plantations to plant food for the savages. They work all day long directing, cutting great jungle trees, clearing out roads, planting crops – Yucca Root, Bananas, Corn, Sugar Cane – to keep the savages in food.

Day after day they come out of the jungles with bleeding hands and feet, tired backs and insect bitten bodies. I saw cuts all over Paul's feet. His wife Tressie, had scars from her knees to her ankles where teesa flies had bitten her, causing inward boils, the core of which go to the bone. It takes at least three months to heal, leaving terrible scars.

The savage is never left alone. While Jack and Paul were in the states on furlough, their father, Thomas Anderson, had charge of the camp. A white man under ordinary conditions would lose his mind in three months. Only God knows the problems. Those missionaries are the greatest pioneering missionaries that have ever lived. The government recognizes the Anderson boys as the finest savage workers and the best linguists in all Bolivia. They both know the Sironois language fluently, speaking it as well as they do English.

Along with the discouraging natural conditions, the Sironois were suspicious and resistant to the Gospel. It took

Jack and Paul Anderson seven years to win their first convert. But interestingly, the greatest discouragement to this missions outreach didn't emerge from the untamed jungles of South America. It wasn't the back–breaking work, or the often–frightening encounters with demonic powers, or the wild animals that nearly broke the Andersons' hearts. But upon their return to the States on Furlough, they were questioned, "How many souls have been saved?" No one understood the incredible challenges that were a part of being faithful to God's call. During that time the Missionary Board considered closing the work – but in the providence of God, did not.

Gradually, the boys made contact with the Sironois and brought them to the Mission Station in Trinidad. On one occasion, Jack brought in a hundred villagers from the bush country to the Christian camp.

It took Jack and Paul seven years to teach the Indians Spanish. But their faithfulness paid off. The same villagers who would think nothing of killing an outsider will drop to their knees to pray in the Spirit, pick up their Spanish Bibles and read as fluently as the boys and girls in the homeland.

DAWN OF A NEW DAY
(FROM THE BOLIVIAN INDIAN MISSIONARY MAGAZINE)

"Jack and Paul Anderson, great in vision, great in heart and great in sacrifice, patiently persisting in unwavering hope, see as it were by the eye of faith, the dawning of a new day when Sironois Savages, men, women and children, shall come out to a saving and transforming experience of Christ, and He is glorified in the midst as all shall own Him and His sovereign sway."

Saying good-bye was very difficult for Harold. He said, "These people fell to the ground weeping, begging me to stay just a few days longer when I left the camp. God got hold of my heart and I buried my heart there, and by the help of God some of these days I am going back to that Savage camp again to preach the gospel."

"TE– TAW"
(THE TALL MAN)

Harold was faithful to his promise and soon God produced wonderful fruit among the Sironois. The natives came to call him "Te–Taw" (the Tall Man). The natives being short in stature – only four to five feet tall – Harold Chalfant must have seemed almost giant–like to them.

But "Te–Taw" lived among the Sironois, adopted their customs, even joined them in their chants and dances. A love grew between "Te–Taw" and the Sironois, a love that God used to bring the people to Christ.

CHAPTER 12
MISSIONARY INSPIRATION

Between missionary trips Harold taught a class on missions at L.I.F.E. Bible College. In preparing the material he studied the biographies of great missionaries from the past. Their lives aroused an interest and excitement that fueled his imagination with a desire to live recklessly and unselfishly for people around the world.

After research and intensive study from available resources, he outlined material and presented it in lecture form to the students. The influence from his words spread like wild fire. Young people were challenged as never before to give their lives to the Lord in total abandonment to His will.

On one occasion, he preached a missionary sermon at Angelus Temple on the theme, "South of the Border." "If you want to be a missionary without portfolio, BE ONE," he thundered. "Just do it! Go a few miles south of the border – find an open area – start preaching…"

"Wherever two roads meet,
I have a pulpit.
If you have to crawl to get there, crawl!
If you have to walk there, walk!
If you have to swim there, swim!
Just Go! The main thing is to get there!"

Many can still remember the appeal of his words as he quoted great men and women of God from the past:

"My human best, filled with the Holy Spirit."

"I do not know anything America needs more today than men and women on fire with the fire of heaven: not great men, but true honest persons God can use."

Dwight Lyman Moody

"Man's extremity is God's opportunity."
That there should be a Christ,
And that I should be Christless;
That there should be a cleansing,
And that I should remain foul;
That there should be a Father's love,
And I should be an alien;
That there should be a heaven,
And I should be cast into hell,
is grief embittered, sorrow aggravated.

Charles H. Spurgeon

"The world has yet to see what God can do with and for and through and in a man who is fully and wholly consecrated to Him."

"Give me souls or I die."

John Knox

When James Calvert went out as a missionary to the cannibal's of the Fiji Islands, the captain of the ship sought to turn him back. "Calvert, you will lose your life and the lives of those with you if you go among such savages," he cried.
Calvert replied, "We died before we came here."
"I will go down, but remember that you must hold the ropes."

William Carey

"I cared not where, or how I lived, or what hardships I went through, so I could gain souls to Christ. While I was asleep I dreamed of those things; and when I awakened, the first thing I thought of was this great work."

David Brainard

The secret of Richard Baxter's life – "He was filled with the Holy Spirit. Baxter would have set the world on fire while another was lighting a match."
"He preached as though he should never preach again, as a dying man to dying men."

Whitfield – True to the symbol on his seal, A winged heart and the inscription, "Astra Petimus" (We seek the stars).

Harold Chalfant's missions class inspired young people to recognize their intrinsic worth and infinite value in the sight of God. As he would often say, "One soul is worth more than the wealth of the world."

All Of Thee

Oh, the bitter pain and sorrow
That a time could ever be
When I proudly said to Jesus
"All of self and none of Thee."
Yet He found me; I beheld Him
Bleeding on the accursed tree,
And my wistful heart said faintly,
"Some of self, and some of Thee."
Day by day His tender mercy
Healing, helping, full and free,
Brought me lower, while I whispered,
"Less of self and more of Thee."
"Higher than the highest heavens,
Deeper than the deepest sea,
Lord, Thy love at last has conquered
"None of self and all of Thee."

Chapter 13
The Last Trip

(Around the World)

At this time... the renewal of Christianity depends solely on accepting the incarnation in all its fullness, for without the realization of God's love for the world, we can neither love the world or God.

Alan W. Watts

Behold the Spirit

For 27 years Harold Chalfant traveled millions of miles, visiting every continent of the world. He became an authority on many isolated tribal groups. The motion pictures he produced won national recognition "Beyond the Bells" is widely acclaimed as a classic work of missionary significance.

Harold spoke to service clubs, high schools and colleges on four continents. At the invitation of Generalisimo and Madame Chiang Kai–shek, Dr. Chalfant spoke to every branch of the armed forces of what was then known as Free China (Taiwan). He spoke to 106,000 troops in Taiwan as well as in 85 public schools.

In the great Orient Crusade, Harold went out to Japan, the Philippines and Okinawa, speaking in the army camps. In Taiwan, he spoke for seven weeks, sixteen times a day, at the Sunrise Schools and army camps. It was an open door for the Gospel of Jesus Christ. Outstanding ministers accompanied him in the Crusades, some of whom included Norman Nelson. Bill Mouer, Lynn Charter and Allan Hamilton. There were other teams that went out about this time, including women's teams.

Perhaps the most inspiring trip Harold took was his final trip around the world. He flew to Europe and down through Africa, to the Indian Ocean. Then he went into Australia to participate in missionary conferences and start youth camps.

In 1959, he went to the island of New Guinea, north of Australia in the South Pacific. Deep in the forests of New Guinea live two million people, representing over 750 language groups. There are over 12,000 villages and thousands of hamlets where the people had never seen a white man. Many, barely out of the stone age, are still practicing cannibalism and head hunting.

When the valley was discovered in 1932, there were estimated to be over 400,000 cannibals in the valley. This valley area, over two hundred miles long and fifty miles wide, is surrounded by a great mountainous range that towers 9,000 to 15,000 feet high.

Rev. and Mrs. Mason Hughes came to New Guinea as missionaries in July, 1956 in an area called Gorka. Mason Hughes spent a year in survey work, looking for a place where the government would grant land for a mission station. At last a location in a wonderful valley about thirty–five miles from Gorka, was chosen. Surrounding this location there are at least fifty villages with no church or mission stations in the vicinity.

During the first year, Mason Hughes took a course in pidgin English and was able to preach in this language. He also learned the local language called "Kafaka", as well as receiving medical training. Through this course he was furnished with medical supplies at no cost. The government also supplied him with school books, free of charge.

Harold spent several weeks with Mason and his family in New Guinea. One day Harold asked Mason. "What in the world ever brought you into this valley among these cannibals?" He said, "Harold, you were speaking in Decatur, Illinois at a convention. On the closing night you gave a missionary call. You said you didn't believe a man had to be called to any one place to preach the gospel, although this definitely happens. You were emphasizing that no matter where we are, or where we go, we preach the gospel and Jesus declares His Word shall not return void. Harold, when you made that challenge, I said to my wife, "Come on honey, let's go down to the altar as candidates. In our case, New Guinea was 'the anywhere'."

Rev. and Mrs. Mason Hughes spent twenty years in New Guinea, even raising their children there. When they left, the local people had come to know Jesus by the tens of thousands.

Chapter 14
935 Kensington Road

Two days before Pearl Harbor, December 5, 1941 Harold, Elsie and their eighteen month old daughter, Joyce, moved into their new home in Los Angeles in the Echo Park District.

The Chalfants loved their home and dedicated it to the glory of God. It became a hospitality center, a home away from home for students, as well as ministers, missionaries, family and friends. Harold took pride in his prolific garden of roses, exotic plants and aviary which he populated with dove and quail.

The basement of his home was converted into a virtual storehouse of priceless artifacts and icons, collected over a period of three decades. The unusual showcase exhibited authentic works of artistic, historical and scientific significance. He showed visitors who came to his home museum thousands of slides and film depicting mission stations around the world.

Harold often said, "Everything about our home is filled with so much love and reminders of our interesting experiences.

Sirinois warriors pose with Harold

"Tee–Taw" (The Tall Man) with the natives

Harold prepares to leave on his first missionary trip

Harold saying goodbye to his family

Harold in the "green hell" of Bolivia

Drinking water out of the jungle swamp in Bolivia

Bolivia: Jack Anderson taking part in a tribal dance

Harold pictured with Sirinois Chiefs

Sirinois Warriors on display

Sirinois Warrior

Harold & his friends

Sirinois Warriors disfigure
their faces

Harold speaking to the troops in Taiwan

Jack Anderson and his sister Rachel

Harold holding a Panamanian baby

Harold looking his
best in Panama

Sirinois warrior in full dress

Map of South America

Trophy room treasures from the mission field

Harold's pride & joy: Living room with polished coffee table & clock

Harold in his garden room among his tropical plants

From New Guinea, I brought home 3,000 spears and arrows from former cannibals. I have three cooking pots that have boiled hundreds of human beings. The cooking pots are hewn, shaped and carved from wood. The shafts on the spears are the longest in the world, many fifteen feet in length."

Harold didn't keep artifacts simply as curiosity, but as illustrations of what the grace of God had done in the lives of some of the most dangerous people in the world. An old chief said to him, "We are different now since the Big Master came into the Valley. He has brought peace to our Valley."

Bus loads of children (often as many as four bus loads at a time) frequented Harold's home to see his museum and participate in a sharing time. The sessions usually took from 2 1/2 to 3 hours. The children were fascinated. They never became tired or bored. Among other things, they were consistently impressed with his huge python skin, stretched out in a cabinet against the wall.

There were many civic groups, as well as individuals from all cultures, creeds and walks of life who visited his home, ranging from superior court judges, lawyers and doctors to high school and college youth.

On several occasions, groups from the Communications Division of the Rand Corporation toured his home. One evening as Harold started showing pictures, a spokesman from the Rand Group said to him, "Harold we will tell you when we want you to stop showing pictures." Harold started his slide presentation at 7:00 PM and stopped at 5:30 AM. Through his slides and film, he had taken his guests on a trip around the world.

Time was running out for Dr. Chalfant. He was acutely aware that his earthly days were numbered. He had many operations, starting with open heart surgery. He had a plastic aorta valve implant and eleven pacemaker implants. He had undergone five knee operations.

The years of active ministry had taken their toll upon him. He had spent himself totally for what he considered to be the highest calling of all, proclaiming the unsearchable riches of Christ Jesus to a lost and dying world. He gave even his last ounce of strength with no regrets.

In his final days he was involved in a Telephone Ministry – touching many lives daily with prayer, comfort and encouragement.

An Optimistic Outlook

In reflecting upon world conditions and the future for all mankind, Harold Chalfant said, "It's going to take strong, dedicated leadership in the next 10 to 20 years, should Jesus tarry. But I believe God has his chosen men and women who will see the work accomplished. It will be a fast work!

"In the early days when we started the youth camps and rallies, this kind of outreach was an entirely new thing – it had never been done before. Today, with evangelism spreading throughout the world through the media of TV, worldwide daily radio broadcasts and satellite transmission, there are millions being reached with the gospel message of Jesus Christ.

"In one telecast, such as the 700 Club and other outstanding broadcasts, we see more lives being touched than we could have ever seen in several lifetimes. What we did see, however, was thrilling, but we haven't seen anything yet. But it's coming. God is in control. Everything is as He has planned.

The future is bright with hope only because of what the power of the Lord Jesus Christ is able to accomplish through any person who is wholly sold out to Him and will dare to live recklessly for God."

How does one write an ending to the life story of Harold George Chalfant? One does not, for the life of "Te–Taw," The Tall Man is unending...

As Goethe the German author said, "I am fully convinced that the soul is indestructible, and that its activity will continue through eternity. It is like the sun, which to our eyes, seems to set in night; but it has in reality gone to diffuse its light elsewhere."

"To live is Christ, to die is gain."
Phil. 1:21

PART III
AN ONGOING MINISTRY

CHAPTER 15
A CIRCLE OF FRIENDS REMEMBERS

M. "BUD" ARGANBRIGHT

Let me tell you what I remember about this dynamic, enthusiastic Christian man Harold Chalfant.

I met Mary Austin and married this wonderful Christian girl while attending the Santa Monica Foursquare Church. After my discharge from the Navy, I continued going to this church in order to play on their softball team. The other players persuaded me to go to summer camp at Radford. So I went up to play ball.

My first glimpse of Harold Chalfant was at the dinner table that first night. After eating his meal, Harold got up on the table, getting the attention of everyone. He proceeded to lay down some rules and the consequences if these rules were broken. He elaborated on the fact that each year a group of "rowdies" waited until the lights were out to start their water and egg throwing antics, disturbing campers who wanted to sleep. Sometimes they broke down doors. Mr. Chalfant went on to caution that there would be a patrol that would deal with the offenders by taking them to the bottom of the hill in San Bernardino, sending them to their homes and not allowing them back in camp.

I didn't hear anything else. I was disgusted. I leaned over to Mary and asked her who this "big boob" thought we were. A bunch of juveniles? After all, I had taken orders for four years in the military service and definitely would not stay in camp all week to listen to such nonsense. I told Mary I was going back down the hill in the morning, but she could stay.

That night, just as the "big boob" had predicted, the rowdiness began. I lay on my cot wondering how some young people could be so juvenile. I also remembered what Harold had said.

The next morning I had a change of heart and surprised Mary by admitting that Harold was 100% right with his prediction. I told her what had happened in my cabin. I decided to stay. Before the week ended, I reconsecrated my life to Jesus Christ. Harold Chalfant became a true friend to me, a man whom I tremendously admired.

Through the years, we developed a friendship like I have never had before or since. I was able to work with Harold during the building of the youth camp at Cedar Crest. We took many trips together; fishing trips on Lake Mead and fabulous elk hunting trips down the Salmon River in Idaho. I would say that every man during his life span should be fortunate enough to have a true friend like Harold Chalfant.

Harold had a favorite poem that was framed and attached permanently to the wall of the chapel at Camp Cedar Crest. I can remember many times when we were up there together, that he would go over to the wall and read the poem to me.

It was so much like Harold and the life he lived for others. I would like to leave it with you.

The Bridge Builder

An old man going a lone highway
Came at evening cold and gray
To a chasm that was vast, and wide, and steep
With waters rolling cold and deep
And the old man crossed in the twilight dim
For this swollen stream held no fear for him

And he paused when safe on the other side
And he built a bridge to span that tide
"Old man," said a fellow pilgrim near
"You're wasting your time with building here
Your journey will end with the passing day
You never again will pass this way
You have crossed the chasm deep and wide"
The builder lifted his gray old head
"Good friend, in the path I have come," he said
"There followeth after me today
A youth whose feet must pass this way
This stream which was naught to me
To that fair lad may a pitfall be
He too must cross in the twilight dim
Good friend, I am building this bridge for him."

HOWARD AND VANEDA COURTNEY

It is often said that "first impressions are lasting ones." So it is with our memories of Harold Chalfant. We first met him in 1935 while we were serving as assistant pastors in the Portland, Oregon Foursquare Church. He was young, vibrant and bubbling over with his burden for young people and his vision for starting youth camping as a national program.

We watched and listened with profound amazement and pledged our participation in his vision. The 135 camps in which we have participated since that time are a testimony to the impact his life and vision had on us.

When we came to headquarters in Los Angeles, as General Supervisor and Director of Foreign Missions, we felt the impact of his life on a day to day basis both in the office and the long telephone calls at night.

It can be truthfully said that multiplied thousands of us are rich in so many, many ways because the Lord sent Harold Chalfant our way. We are proud to have known him as a friend and a lifetime co-worker in the great cause of the Lord, Jesus Christ, whom he loved passionately.

EDYTHE DORRANCE

The genius of Harold Chalfant's life was that he was touched by the love of God and set aflame by the inspiration of the Holy Spirit! When Harold's love and concern surfaced for the youth of our movement, we were delighted as we were already involved with a missionary program and burden for expansion. Dr. Dorrance and I were invited to share Harold's enthusiasm. We drove all over the San Bernardino Mountains looking for a camp site. Finally we found the location for Camp Cedar Crest.

Subsequently, mass rallies were conducted all over Southern California in which many thousands of dollars were raised to purchase the property and start building. I remember giving my personal inheritance from my father to have a road built from the highway to the camp. It wouldn't seem like much today, but $500 then, equated a tidy sum of money. It was like that everywhere. People gave unselfishly and sacrificially for a cause they believed in – God honored our faith.

The inspiration and influence of Harold Chalfant's life continues to touch lives today. We see this evidence in the "Circle of Friends" group.

LELAND AND BARBARA EDWARDS

Soon after Harold had been appointed by Aimee Semple McPherson as International President of Youth, he started the Foursquare Crusader Missionary Program in 1937. Some of the first that were appointed were MK's (missionary children) Paul, Rachel and Jack Anderson in Bolivia, Rhenna Adams in Puerto Rico, and Donald and Leland Edwards in Panama.

I received my appointment in April of 1937, two months before graduating from high school in Panama. Although the starting salary was $25.00, it provided the open door for Foursquare Youth to minister abroad.

In the United States, the Foursquare Crusader movement grew very fast. Great train rallies were held in Ventura and Santa Barbara. Youth Camps were started at Camp Radford and later spread to other areas. Harold's office published the Crusader Manual – full of ideas for youth programs and news of the happenings in the Crusader Movement.

On the field in Panama, I read of these endeavors – especially the Camps. We published in Spanish the Crusader Manual for our Crusaders and in 1939 held our first Crusader Camp in the interior of Panama. The whole program was patterned after that at Radford, even including skit night. Our camp in 1939 was the first evangelical youth camp south of the Rio Grande. Camp was an immediate success and it was not long before we were conducting five camps a year in our little country.

Toward the end of the decade of the 1930's, Harold and Elsie came to Panama. He was on his way to Bolivia, on his first trip to visit Foursquare Mission fields. They spoke in several meetings in Panama, after which Harold went south and Elsie returned to Los Angeles. This was the beginning of his many trips to the mission fields. It was Harold who first brought a very vivid presentation of missions to U. S. churches. His $35.00 Keystone movie camera did wonders, producing black and white films that, along with his very gifted speaking, inspired pastors and members alike to become interested in missions. Quite a number were called to be missionaries and several served in the field.

In 1940, while on furlough, I had the privilege of spending much time with Harold in missionary conferences and youth services. But, it wasn't until 1945 that I attended a camp in the U. S. It was the Camp at Radford. The experience added to our abilities in the ministry of youth on the foreign field.

HAZEL HARRY

Harold and Elsie have a very special place in my heart, not only because of their encouragement during the sad times, but also in the good times. They inspired me to walk closely with God.

I met Roy, my husband, in 1940 while singing in the Glee Club at Angelus Temple. I attended Camp Radford the next summer for the first time.

Roy and I were married in November, 1941. The war started in December. Roy enlisted in the Air Force. Just before he left for training, Harold baptized the both of us at Angelus Temple. We were his first baptismal candidates.

Harold inspired us to become vitally interested in missions. During that time Harold raised funds to purchase the Cedar Crest property, my entire family, H.D. Nogle and Sons Contractors, helped in the construction of the camp.

When my husband died in 1982, Harold called and kept in touch with me to encourage me. When my daughter Joanie became terminally ill in 1988, Harold was the one she wanted to see. He not only ministered to her in her illness, but also stayed in close contact, helping me get through some of the most difficult days of my life.

LEONARD AND MARJORIE HARVEY

As acting coordinators of the Circle of Friends group of over 300 members, Marjorie and I are acutely aware of the tremendous and lasting ministry of Harold Chalfant. Most of our members found Christ as their Lord and Savior in the Foursquare denomination when Harold served as International Director of Youth. So many were called into ministry as a direct result of Harold's challenge to "Live Recklessly for Christ."

As a result of Marjorie's work in the International Youth Office, we were privileged to work very closely with Harold at Camp Radford, then in the formative days of Camp Cedar Crest where we participated in the giant Missionary Boom Barrel Rallies, where we were able to observe his strong drive and dedication. He was intensely competitive, willing to give his all, and very impatient with anyone else who gave less.

We are reminded of the Apostle Paul when we think of the ministry of Harold Chalfant. Like Paul, Harold was devoted to preaching the Word of God. He, like Paul, made many missionary journeys and knew how to be content in times of need or plenty.

We are pleased to know that Harold's life will be chronicled and commemorated in "Out of the Flame" for it was "Out of the Flame" of those Victory Circle fires that hundreds of lives were dedicated to the cause of Christ. Thousands of lives were snatched "Out of the Flame" of the eternal fires of Hell, as a result of Harold's presentation relative to the claims of Christ.

We loved him dearly and still miss him.

JACK HAYFORD

Harold Chalfant was very encouraging toward me during the years I served as National Youth Director of our movement. By this time he was already gone from the ministerial role in our denomination, but would occasionally call me with kind words of affirmation when he heard of the things I was doing.

When he spoke to me at the premiere of "Majesty" his words were very assuring that I was "on track" in the spirit of our founder. His specific words about my ministry the night "Majesty" was presented were that he felt what I was doing was not only consonant with, but in the same stream and advancing of the same spirit that was upon the ministry of Sister McPherson. Very moving words indeed.

I rise with gratitude to God for Harold's anointed ministry. His friendship shown toward me is a treasured memory.

HAROLD AND WINONA HELMS

We were both in our teens as we sat in Angelus Temple during a convention and watched this energetic, forceful speaker pace back and forth on the platform. He was driven by his desire to reach the countries of South America. He had been there and the word pictures he drew were impacting.

Just as he moved the hearts of men and women that night, he also stirred and kindled a fire in the hearts of many youth to prepare and give their lives for ministry. I was one of those he touched.

The old preachers' adage. "I'd rather burn out than rust out," could certainly apply to Harold Chalfant. His life was one of burning, restless zeal. That zeal touched our lives.

RONALD HOLCOMB

Harold Chalfant was a gifted man who was uniquely used by the Lord to bless many lives. Only eternity will reveal the multitude of souls that his life touched in leading them to commit their lives to service in God's Kingdom.

Harold's ability to communicate his faith to others was tremendously effective. He forcefully conveyed the urgency of total commitment to Christ as the greatest decision anyone could ever make.

His energy and zeal were unflagging. On one occasion I drove with him as we held meetings in Foursquare Churches in the South. Sometimes we drove day and night in order to maintain his schedule. He was never too tired to witness for Christ, nor was there any loss of vigor or inspiration in his speaking.

He was a generous person. After we left our pastorate in Little Rock, Arkansas, to teach in L.I.F.E. Bible College, he invited my wife Mildred and me to live in his home for a time.

Harold loved a good joke. One morning after teaching in the Bible College, I got into my car, started the engine, then put it in gear. Nothing happened. The automobile did not move. Why? Well, because Harold had jacked up a rear wheel. He had a rare sense of humor.

HAROLD JEFFRIES

Our organization was ready for something more; then God gave us Harold Chalfant. We did have our Crusader youth program, initiated by Sister Aimee Semple McPherson and our youth rallies all over the nation, but we did not have a camping program. Harold emerged upon the scene when our Youth Program in the Foursquare movement was in it's infancy.

Harold was a man of inspiration and influence. His keen mind and deep sense of purpose inspired youth to a measure of dedication that eternity alone will reveal.

As supervisor of the Northwest district, I remember our first camp, before we owned a camp of our own. Harold came to us as the Holy Spirit began forming his ministry among the youth. When he preached he was able to inspire the young people to believe in Jesus and His greatness. He showed them that the life worth living was one dedicated to the cause of Christ.

During those times the call of God hung like a mist over the services at camp. The urgency of the Spirit was to answer the call of God while you were young.

Harold perceived the training and equipping of youth as the answer to the spiritual needs of the Church, and particularly so on the mission field. By his enthusiasm and unique ideas, he raised literally thousands of dollars for missions. Who will ever forget his "Boom Barrel", or "Dollar Nights" at youth rallies or conventions.

Every camp came to have a victory circle. There, in the twilight hours of a summer day, the young people gathered to sing and give their testimonies of victories won. The camps ended with a Commitment service. As the young people sat or stood around the camp fire, with the glow from the fire in their faces and the glow of God's Spirit in their hearts, each would throw a pine cone into the fire and watch as it was consumed in the flame. The fire represented the consuming fire of God. Many a stubborn will would be broken at this time.

But Harold never forgot that young people needed their moments of fun too. In the middle of the week, Skit Night was presented. Harold with his side-kick, Ulphin Davis, assisted by a local pastor or supervisor, would put on some of the most outlandish skits, leaving the audience weak with laughter.

As I reflect upon the life of Harold Chalfant, I can visualize hundreds of youth responding to Christ, offering themselves to Him as their "reasonable service." (Romans 12:1)

JERRY JENSEN

During the years I first attended Camp Radford, I was interested only in the sports program and "camp dates." But each night at Victory Circle the Lord gained an inroad to my heart. Finally, one pivotal year on Friday night, I threw my cone in the fire and committed my life to full–time service for the Lord.

During those early camp years I don't think Harold hardly knew who I was. He only knew I was Elwood Jensen's brother. Elwood was editor of the camp paper and my only claim to fame. Little did Harold know the influence he had on my life at that time.

My commitment to full–time service brought me to L.I.F.E. Bible College and while there I finally became personally acquainted with Harold Chalfant. It happened my second year at L.I.F.E.. I attended a crusader rally at Angelus Temple. Harold spoke and as a result of his dynamic message, I responded to the call for commitment. That night I introduced myself to Earle Williams who was Angelus Temple's youth pastor. I told him of my commitment and desire to do youth work. As a result, my wife–to–be Helen Levine and I became part of the Angelus Temple youth staff, and our first official appointment at graduation was to be assistant youth leaders of Angelus Temple.

Harold's charisma made it the desire of almost every L.I.F.E. graduate to be a district youth director. There were only seven districts in the USA so the possibilities were very limited. But God worked a miracle for Helen and me and we were appointed directors of Youth and Christian Education for the Gulf States District. We were finally working directly with Harold Chalfant. He was guest speaker at our camps and district rallies and we learned to love and appreciate the talent and dedication of this special man.

Harold came to one of our district conventions and gave a missionary appeal. When he finished his message and challenged us to give I thought to myself, I have only twenty dollars but I know Helen has twenty also, so I'll give all I have and we can get to our next meeting with her money. The problem was that Helen was sitting across the auditorium from me and she decided to give all she had because she knew I had traveling money. We compared notes at the close of the service and found that we were flat broke. However, as Harold always said, "You can't out–give God..." Later that same evening someone, we don't remember who, gave me an envelope and inside was forty dollars cash.

You have read in many of the testimonies in this book about Harold's famous "Boom Barrel" teams. I traveled on the second team with Dr. Earl Dorrance and missionary Claude Updike throughout Central and South America where we witnessed first hand the tremendous need for the gospel throughout the world. Like so many of Harold's projects, they were "double–barreled." The effect was equally as strong on the giver as it was on the receiver. No matter how many times I have ministered in various parts of the world, I will never forget how Harold's missionary project: "The Boom Barrel Missionary Teams" kindled a missionary fire in my heart.

After our work in the Gulf States District we were asked to come to Headquarters and work in the national youth office. Needless to say, working with Harold Chalfant on a day–to–day basis was a polishing process that has helped us in our years with Youth For Christ and now with Full Gospel Business Men's Fellowship International.

HELEN JENSEN

In June 1937, our family moved to Randsburg, California. My parents, Rev. & Mrs. Levine, were sent to pastor that tiny church. The young people were getting excited about Camp Radford. My brother Art, my sister Doris and I were all teenagers and pretty sure the $15.00 each was impossible on my dad's $5.00 weekly salary. I still don't know how, but God provided the money miraculously for all three of us to go to Radford with the rest.

We had so much fun, enjoyed so many activities and met so many friends. But the best memory was of Harold Chalfant, the camp director, who on Friday night at a meeting around a huge campfire, challenged us to burn out our lives for God. One by one we threw our pine cones in the fire and dedicated our lives to do whatever He would call us to do. There is no way of knowing how many hearts have been touched through those Friday night victory circle challenges.

Not only I, but many other young people went to L.I.F.E. to prepare for whatever the Lord had called them to do. Jerry Jensen and I met there and married and together fulfilled the call of God in youth work. There were years that we, too, conducted summer camps all around the south, and were privileged to have Harold as our guest on many occasions. And with that same challenge, we were rededicated to giving ourselves and our talents and our meager means to His cause.

We still think of Harold Chalfant as one of God's greatest men to lead young people to sell out to Christ in every work of the Lord, both at home and in every part of the world.

We say with thousands of others: What a legacy he has left for the gospel of Christ and all of those he influenced through the years!

JOANN JOHNSON

The man was magnetic! As a thirteen year old girl, I was impressed with his looks, his dynamo and his love for God. My father, too, was handsome, but he was not a Christian nor did he live in our home. So as I look back in retrospect, I realize Harold Chalfant not only influenced my life for Christ, but fulfilled my need for what is commonly known as a "father figure" in today's world.

I remember one incident that meant so much to me as a thirteen year old girl. Harold was guest speaker at the Hawthorne Foursquare Church, which was located one block from the main drag. After church, Harold took a few young people to the soda fountain . I got to sit on the stool right next to him. It was a special moment that I will never forget.

The rich spiritual blessings that I received from the camp totally changed the direction of my life: One of my favorite nights was "skit night." Harold's humor was fantastic – he was truly a comedian and knew how to have loads of fun.

Harold's heart was tender toward God. To me, he passed on a legacy of desire to be fully dedicated to God, and I will always thank God for the times I can still "toss my pine cone into the Victory Circle fire of my life" and renew my devotion to my Lord.

Harold's life was the catalyst for thousands of young people and his flame will never die for it was ignited by God himself.

VIRGINIA KINDT

Harold Chalfant was a man with an insatiable desire to bring young people into a focused position in their lives. During the peak of his ministerial career as International Director of Youth and Christian Education, he influenced thousands of young people to experience a real spiritual awakening. The varied paths these young people have taken range from ministers to lay people in the Foursquare denomination, and other affiliations such as World Opportunities, Calvary Chapels, Presbyterian, Baptist, Assembly of God, et cetera. His influence was not limited.

I worked with Harold Chalfant for thirteen years starting at the age of seventeen. I found working for Harold was a very rewarding experience. He felt that in living and working for Christ there should be a recklessness, fervency, sincerity and lack of doubt in one's mind as to what should be the ultimate goal.

Harold stressed youth, camps, and missions. He went to all peoples, nationalities, and any who wanted to work for Christ and the Church. If there was a young person in need, he was always there to see this need was met. He felt as if this one young person might change the destinies of other lives, and this has been proven with many of the young people he influenced.

Harold knew that no man was perfect, but he felt as if the vision, thoughts and works would all blend together in producing a great man. He did not believe that success for Christ in your life was handed to you on a "silver platter" but that you must work for that success with fervor.

ALAN LAMB

I first met Harold Chalfant during the last years of Camp Radford. I knew nothing about God at that time, but when I went to camp Harold stirred my heart with his dynamic messages. To me he was the most exciting, exuberant speaker I had ever heard. Every time he spoke, I would go to the altar.

Thinking back, I realize that he touched thousands of lives, while they in turn touched thousands of lives – like a huge snow ball rolling on and on. It's a thrill for me to see many of those lives going on in service for the Lord.

A few years ago I went back to Camp Radford for a Harold Chalfant reunion. There I had an opportunity to become reacquainted with him again. Since he could not drive because of physical limitations he asked me to drive him back home to Los Angeles. Not being too familiar with the roads I asked Harold for directions about a half mile from camp. He instructed me to turn down a certain road and I told him that I thought it was the wrong way. He assured me he had traveled that way a thousand times before. I followed his leading only to end up on a dead end. He said, "They must have put trees in the way."

ART AND JOY LARSON, JR.

I was fourteen years old when I first met Harold Chalfant at the Northwest District Youth Camp in 1936 at Trestle Glen near Portland, Oregon. I went to camp with a group of Crusaders from the Coos Bay, Oregon Foursquare church. At that time Ulphin and Emma Davis were the camp directors. Harold Chalfant was featured guest speaker for morning classes and evening services. On the last night, Harold led the inspiring Victory Circle where we threw our pine cones into the fire. It was on that memorable night that I consecrated my life to the Lord – for a life time of service, wherever God would lead me. Harold Chalfant next influenced me while a student at L.I.F.E. Bible College, where he taught a class on missions.

My wife, Joy, was fifteen when she first met Harold Chalfant at the Midwest District Conclaves in Omaha, and Chattanooga. She thought his morning classes on Science and the Bible were fabulous. The classes helped strengthen her faith as a teenager, particularly at a crucial time when secular education was questioning the existence of God. Harold's missionary sermons were exciting and inspirational. His unique rapport on a personal basis made Joy and her friends feel like they were Harold's important friends.

In the summer of 1944, six months after we were married, we became Midwest District Youth Directors. We began a close working relationship with Harold Chalfant, our "boss." Just observing Harold in action was an education.

Not only were we inspired by his missionary vision and passionate preaching, but we learned from his example that organization, promotion, and planning ahead are also important factors in being a successful leader.

Annie La Voire

When I first heard Harold preach I was sixteen years old. He spoke on missions and had many artifacts on display which he had brought back from some of the mission fields. How well I remember my feelings that night, I was frightened of the challenge, yet willing if that was God's will for my life. I also remember saying, "But please Lord, don't let me go where they have so many snakes and spiders."

Upon graduating from high school, I won the coveted chance to be interviewed as an apprentice designer for Hollywood Sports Life. I got the job. What a thrill! I was on my way!

I heard Harold speak many times and each time I felt a strong desire to serve the Lord in a more dedicated way. I started L.I.F.E. Bible College, attending night classes. I thought if I could just be a real good Sunday School teacher I would be happy.

Up until this time I had not attended summer camp. Now that I was working I went to Camp Radford. What a thrill and what a challenge! The Victory Circle was a time of tears for me and again as Harold led us in singing the beautiful hymn "I'll go where you want me to go, dear Lord," I dedicated my life anew.

In 1942, I married an upper class student by the name of Norman Smith. When he graduated we left Los Angeles to pastor the El Paso, Texas Foursquare Church. Next we moved to Dallas, Texas where my husband was the Crusader Commander of the Gulf States District. Harold Chalfant was the International Youth Director for the Foursquare organization and we worked under his direction.

In 1946, the Missionary Board gave us the opportunity to go to Puerto Rico as missionaries. Puerto Rico has a rainy season and a dry season, both hot. This caused health problems and we had to return home. Though my life changed, God had chosen a different course for me while I was young and able to go where He wanted me to go. Harold Chalfant had a lasting affect on my life.

CARL LUCHT

As an instrument of God, Harold Chalfant was used in organizing the international youth programs, known as Foursquare Crusaders. He started the camping programs, the mass youth rallies and projected his tremendous burden for missions. As an instructor at L.I.F.E. Bible College, Harold vividly portrayed the challenge of missions as he reviewed the lives of missionary heroes.

When he first began his mission trips to Bolivia, Panama, New Guinea, and other countries. – he would return home displaying his impressive collection of artifacts and pictures. The experiences he related never ceased to challenge us.

The camping program at Camp Seeley and Camp Radford literally touched thousands of young people. The in–depth Bible teaching, recreational programs and evangelistic services, as well as skit night and Victory Circle are still very much alive in my memory.

In 1944, God called Maxine and I to the China field. At the time of our calling, we were sitting on opposite sides of the church at the mass Boom Barrel rally in Long Beach, California.

MAXINE LUCHT

I recall the first time I met Harold, We passed in the "tunnel" between L.I.F.E. Bible college building and Angelus Temple. I was eighteen and a long way from home. His warm welcome to L.I.F.E. meant a lot to me. It was the fall semester, 1940.

For a period before I graduated I enjoyed working in Harold's office. I'm sure his passion for souls and foreign missions fervor had a definite impact on my life, as did his leadership at Camp Radford and Cedar Crest.

Harold visited Carl and me and our children in the mission fields of both Japan and Hong Kong. He displayed great empathy following my first spinal surgery in Hong King and insisted that I needed to get home at the close of our fourth year, second term. He loyally backed us in our adoption of our daughter, Jennifer.

TOM MATTHEWS

Harold knew the value of humor in the camping program. He realized that we cannot give young people a restricted diet of spiritual things and expect them to live well adjusted balanced lives.

Along with classes on the Bible, preaching and times of prayer, Harold incorporated planned recreation and organized sports such as ball games, swimming competition, hiking, crafts – and humor. He used humor to show young Christians that Christianity is not a dull, boring life.

For example, at lunch time in the dining hall. Harold would give out the mail. He would read a postcard from a parent to a teenage daughter as though the card came from a love–sick boyfriend, adding words to the card that weren't actually there. This brought laughter, as well as good–natured embarrassment to the young lady. And in the dining hall there would be fun singing songs such as: "That's a lot of applesauce." There was laughter and camaraderie.

But the humor highlight of the week was "Skit Night." Young people would originate and present a skit, designed, of course, to bring laughter. And, along with mistakes in the presentation such as forgetting lines, props falling down or, some other "disaster," it only added to the fun.

The youngsters who attended camp under the leadership of Harold Chalfant are now "oldsters." But they still love to talk about going to camp. The spiritual lessons learned in those camps have never been forgotten.

One of the best lessons I learned in working with Harold was the lesson that God will use us if we are willing to be used. It has been over fifty years since I first attended a camp under Harold Chalfant. I still go to camp. Thanks, Harold.

ROY MCKEOWN

It was the time of the Great Depression in America. Our house in Olympia, Washington was small, but worth the $8.00 rent per month. Our furniture was old, and there wasn't much food on the table, but we were thankful for what we had.

Because my dad was the pastor of the local Foursquare Church, he and my mother often entertained visiting missionaries in our home. This meant giving up my bed, but I never minded when Harold came. He always had so many fascinating stories to tell about far–away places such as Bolivia, Africa and China. I'll never forget his stories about the lepers in Africa. He was a marvelous story teller; he could make me laugh, make me cry, and make me yearn to see the places he had been. And while he had us all mesmerized at our dining room table, he never failed to compliment my mother on her cooking. I started attending summer camp at the Crusader Camp Trestle Glen. For several years I listened to Harold as he challenged me and other campers about the need to commit our lives to Jesus Christ in total abandonment to His express will.

I committed my life to full–time service, along with my bride Marianne, at Camp Radford, as we threw our pine cones into the roaring campfire and watched as they were consumed by flames (representing our dedication to the Holy Spirit's consuming fire in our lives). We have been involved in Christian work ever since.

I vividly recall the words I spoke to Harold as he visited me in my office at World Opportunities: "Thanks, Harold for all you have meant in my life – from those early days in Olympia, to the Crusader Camp, to my college days."

His encouragement played a major role in my working with world missions. A great deal of my responsibilities in Third World Countries and as President of World Opportunities International can be attributed to the days when he challenged me to live 'recklessly' for Jesus Christ…the meaning of which was to commit my life fully to serving our Lord and Savior – never counting the cost.

Harold Chalfant challenged me through "tough love" to serve God in those early camp days. During that time of dedication, I took as one of my life's Scriptures: "For to me, living means opportunities for Christ." (Philippians 1:21 Living Bible)

DEAN MILLER

Our lives are shaped and influenced by others. Harold Chalfant had a great impact on my life. During my teen years I attended Camp Radford and vividly recall this dynamic man as he challenged me, especially during Victory Circle, to commit my life to Jesus Christ as Lord and Savior.

I can still hear his call to "live recklessly for Christ!" He showed love for a skinny kid who grew up in the Echo Park area, and patience for my faltering discipleship.

I, who had never traveled on an airplane, or out of the United States was enthralled when Harold would describe his missionary journeys in graphic language and speak of the great commission to go "into all the world and preach the gospel." This instilled in me a love for mission outreach which

I have emphasized throughout my life as a Presbyterian minister.

Harold was a great communicator. He possessed the God–given gift of being able to persuade and move people with his impassioned speech. Through the years we continued to be dear friends and later it was my privilege to minister to him.

"Bud" Vernon Nogle

During the summer of 1942 between my junior and senior years in high school, I first became acquainted with Harold. That particular summer all the weeks of camp were filled and it looked like I would not be able to go.

At the end of the camping season, however, Harold decided to have over–flow camp, which I attended along with 86 other young people. We received a challenge to "live for Christ." Many times I have thought back to that week at summer camp.

In January, 1946, I was discharged from the service. That summer I was back in camp thanking Him for all He had done for me in the service. I met Betty Jo Boyer, my wife to be, at that camp. Betty had attended every year from the time she was old enough to go. After Betty Jo and I married we spent many weeks and months working at Camp Cedar Crest. To see it develop from year to year reaching tens of thousands of youth for Christ, was richly rewarding in terms of eternal values.

Today our children and grandchildren have been blessed by the camping program and Harold's vision and dedication.

Betty Jo Nogle

As a youngster in 1937, I attended the Santa Monica Foursquare Church. I remember attending the tremendous train rallies, the missionary "Boom Barrel" rallies, camp and other exciting youth programs under the direction of Harold Chalfant. The planned activities laid a firm foundation in developing my life and allowing the Lord to take control of it.

I thank the Lord for Harold's leadership and his love for missions. He instilled within us a desire to serve the Lord. People of all ages loved him. I know that our generation was better because of Harold Chalfant.

WAYNE AND RUTH NOGLE

Harold often said, "Don't rust out," and, "It's better to burn out for God."

In his early days the camping program was his primary concern. More than any other person, Harold Chalfant was instrumental in building the camps and successful programs. As youth from the Norwalk, California church we went to Camp Radford. Our lives were enriched by it.

Words cannot say what an influence he was to our lives. He truly committed his life to Christ and served him to the fullest. Only eternity will reveal the way lives were changed by his knowledge of the Bible and excellent way in which he explained God's universe; the planets – the stars – and the grandeur of the heavens. No one was able to present God's plan for our lives as Harold could. He made it all so real and believable. Surely there will be many stars in his crown for all the souls that were saved.

Many young people were called to the mission fields because of his enthusiasm and sincerity, He loved the foreign field and was an inspiration to the young missionaries when he visited them.

My brothers, Lloyd and Leslie, and sister Velma have been serving for forty two years on the mission field, mostly in Brazil. They were influenced much by Camp Radford and Camp Cedar Crest.

A highlight in our memory was Victory Circle when we all gathered around the great fire ring. We made honest commitments to the Lord. It was very meaningful as each of us threw our pine cone into the big fire. Only God shared our secret. Only He knew what the pine cone represented.

BARNEY NORTHCOTE

I knew Harold Chalfant as a man with a burning passion in two specific areas of Christian ministry; youth and world missions. Harold brought a new and fresh concept to Christian Youth Camps. His driving intensity in these two areas of ministry led to bold, innovative ideas that expanded in outreach, encompassing the world. Of course, there was work being done for youth in this respect, but the Harold Chalfant concept found overwhelming success in challenging youth to give total dedication to Christian service.

At a time when atheism was on the rise, his brilliant studies on Science and the Bible, from which his sermons were compiled, had an enormous impact on young audiences, with widespread results. I can still hear him saying, "Can you imagine what would happen to an orange if you put it in your pocket, to discover that it was covered with the peeling of an apple?" God designed the apple and the orange uniquely, each with appropriate skin. Just picture this if the skins were reversed.

The Harold Chalfant story deserves a place in 20th Century Christian literature. I am proud of the work that has been done in producing "Out of the Flame."

JIM AND MARY LOU RITCH

Harold's ability to challenge youth for Christ was amazing. He possessed the heartbeat of a missionary and motivated many thousands to give, pray and go for the cause of Jesus Christ.

In the summer of 1943 I met Mary Lou. I was sitting in the large dining room of camp with a bunch of guys and across the aisle, there she was. I said to my friend, "Hey, I'm going to marry that cute little girl some day." We all had a good laugh.

Later, a mutual friend introduced us to each other. She said she was from Escondido California. "Escondido! Where's that?" I said. My turf was Hollywood and the Sunset Strip.

After camp I didn't see Mary Lou again until I was stationed in San Diego, California with the Navy. At the summer camp of 1945 I joined with the Escondido Youth Group for a weekend. The camp was a great one, and God performed a very special work in my heart.

Back in Escondido, during the camp echoes service in church, God called me into full time ministry – and Mary Lou was willing to go with me. It was my privilege to serve on the camp staff for 30 years. I'm still on the board of directors.

One of the buildings at Cedar Crest is known as the Chalfant Auditorium. Quite often people come to me and ask me about the "man" the auditorium was named for. I tell them that he was "the man of the hour for our generation and that he traveled around the world proclaiming the unsearchable riches of Jesus Christ."

Mary Lou and I are just retiring from 42 years of pastoral ministry; 32 years of which were spent as Senior Pastors of the La Peunte California Foursquare Church. God was gracious in giving us many precious souls for our life–long service. A vision for missions was implanted and birthed in our hearts because of the life and inspiration of Harold Chalfant.

RUTH SMITH

As a teenager during World War II in 1946, I was born again at Camp Radford. The next summer at camp, seated around the Victory Circle fire ring, I remember Harold saying, "If just one of you kids goes home and serves the Lord all year, I'll blow a gasket."

The Holy Spirit used that unconventional challenge to inspire my teenage heart. From that point on, my life changed. "I'll be that person," I determined, "I'll live for Jesus," and next year when I come back to camp, I'll tell him about it."

I returned to camp the following summer bringing my two sisters and a girl friend from high school with me. All three girls were led to Christ and challenged to live dedicated lives. Life touching life. That's what it is all about.

After the summer camps there were the mass Crusader rallies in the fall. Held at Angelus Temple, these rallies attracted tens of thousands of teens. As the inspirational "mouth piece", Harold passed the vision on to receptive hearts, my own included.

My husband Paul and I are in the ministry today because of God's anointing upon the life of Harold Chalfant. God used his dynamic personality to speak to youth in a way that really moved upon their hearts.

Down through the years he always greeted me as "dimples," warm and friendly. I believe he must have recognized that God had used him to touch another life in touching mine, and the beautiful part was that he was able to witness the fruit of his ministry going on.

DON STAUFFER

I was 13 years old and had just become a Christian. My heart was filled with joy and a burning desire to serve the Lord, when I was invited to attend a youth meeting at the San Diego Foursquare Church and that was when I had my first encounter with Harold Chalfant. He had come to promote summer camps at Radford.

I immediately decided that I wanted to go to camp. Little did I realize that I would spend the next 19 years of my life being an integral part of the Radford experience and have the extraordinary opportunity of assisting Harold Chalfant in the great camping program.

I became a part of a highly competitive softball program that was started by Ulphin Davis. Later Ulphin could not participate and I was appointed the camp sports director. Sometimes our games became highly competitive. Not only the campers, but our missionaries, and organizational leaders became involved in the softball games.

I remember an incident at camp that involved me personally. During a championship softball game, I slid into home plate. The camp guest of the day was Aimee Semple McPherson. When I picked myself up, Sister McPherson called me over and said, "Boy, if you will preach the Gospel like you play baseball you will go somewhere!" Her words stimulated a desire in me to enter the ministry and later I enrolled as a student at L.I.F.E Bible College.

During the Radford years and the construction of Camp Cedar Crest, Harold and I became very close friends. The wonderful memories of camp, the tremendous youth rallies, the great missionary endeavors by Harold were celebrated in four memorable reunions which brought hundreds of the Radford alumni from all over the world.

LEITA MAE STEWARD

"Dare to live recklessly for God", "Walk the second mile with God" and "Be a gambler for God" were the challenging messages the Lord emblazoned deep within my heart through His servant, Dr. Harold Chalfant. "Let Go and Let God live in You in All His Fullness" came across loud and clear. I can't begin to tell you what a fire was kindled within my soul through his dynamic messages at Camp Cedar Crest and then in his Sunday School Class.

My sister, Roberta Harris, and I first attended Camp Radford in 1935. What an encounter with life and vision! Through selling donuts, putting on a community play and personal sacrifice, we were able to bring approximately sixty young people to camp. A Foursquare Church was founded with events for the youth.

I was at Camp Radford in 1942. Through tears, I answered God's call to go to L.I.F.E. Bible College – to leave home and all the securities I had known, to wholeheartedly give Him my all. Truly camp, under Harold's direction, was my place of inspiration and blessing.

Soon after entering Bible College the Lord miraculously confirmed His will for me to work at the Headquarters of the International Church of the Foursquare Gospel – this confirmation was made real to me through the scriptures in I Chronicles 28:20–21. As of April 5,1993, I have spent fifty wonderful years of ministry as Executive Secretary.

I can never thank God enough for Harold who challenged me to triumphantly follow God regardless of circumstances. He also challenged all of us to give, not only our lives, but our money to God. He truly lived his declaration, "I want to be a gambler for God until the day I die."

When Harold was speaking, the Lord spoke to me to give every dime I had. In the meantime, I had moved away from home and was living from payday to payday. I gladly gave everything to missions that night. In a couple of days I was combing my hair getting ready for work when I said, "Lord, there is a need in my life and You will have to meet it." In a matter of minutes I was walking to work in Victorville and in the middle of the street was a crisp $5.00 bill.

BERT TEAFORD

I knew Harold Chalfant as a teenager and pioneer in our youth group known as Foursquare Crusaders. It all started in 1926 when I was a new convert, having accepted Christ at the altar in Angelus Temple. I was 18 years of age and Harold was about 14.

The big revival hit Angelus Temple in 1923 with many thousands of youth converted. Harold was caught up by the excitement and enthusiasm of the youth. With his boundless vim and vitality, he exercised his ability as an expert bean shooter in tormenting Mrs. Hinderlighter who was a "Lady Orderly" appointed to discipline the youth who got out of line. It was about that time that God got a hold of Harold and caused him to dedicate his life to Christ.

Before the birth of the Crusader Organization, the youth group at Angelus Temple was known as the "Foursquare League". The officers were Roberta Semple, Hubert Mitchell, Ada Artmenkle, George Johnson and myself. Later, when sister McPherson renamed the League "The Foursquare Crusaders", she appointed Harold as Southern California Commander.

During the time I pastored the Long Beach church, Sister McPherson asked me to organize a summer camp program for

the California District. Our first camp was held in Camp
Seeley. The next year I suggested that she appoint Harold
Chalfant as the Director. I felt Harold showed promising signs
of becoming a great International Crusader Commander.
Harold directed Camp Radford the following year and subsequently built Camp Cedar Crest. He inspired vision to all the
districts to have their own camps.

I knew and worked with Harold for over 60 years, from the
time he first accepted Christ. He was a great guy... and I am
sure the Lord will say to him, "Well done, thou good and
faithful servant. Enter thou into the joy of thy Lord."

EVELYN THOMPSON

For sometime I had watched Harold Chalfant from afar at
Angelus Temple, recognizing the unique anointing upon his
life and ministry. Being a bit shy, it was difficult to become
acquainted and allow myself to be known. However, I loved
the youth work.

My earnest interest in Camp Radford came in 1934. I
learned to know Harold and Elsie by helping the staff in its
various activities. My husband was happy for the opportunities I was given to minister. This brought me into a pleasant
fellowship and lasting friendship with Harold, which brought
about my appointment as Youth Missionary Commander of
the Southern California District.

When our personal "house of dreams" crumbled, it was
Harold Chalfant who continued to encourage my husband and
me. One year at camp I remember singing, "Take everything
but my Lord." When I came to the part in the song that says,
    "...Take my reputation,
    my dearest blood relation,
    The sunshine, the flowers and the birds..."

I broke, losing my voice, choked with tears. It was Harold
who stood behind me, urging me to go on. I could not under-
stand my feelings until a few weeks later when I watched our
beautiful little daughter leave this world to be at home with

The Bevers Family

Bert Teaford

Mr. & Mrs. Loren Wood

Earle E. Williams

Tom. Matthews

Jerry Jensen

Clarence Hall

Lester & Hope Vollmer

Bud & Betty Joe Nogle

Joann Johnson

Bud & Mary Arganbright

Annie LaVoire

Dean Miller

Barney Northcote

Edythe Dorrance

Leita Mae Steward

Joy & Art Larson

Dr. & Mrs.
Harold Jeffries

Karl & Leona Williams

Dr. & Mrs.
Howard P. Courtney

Leonard & Marjorie
Harvey

Wayne & Ruth Nogle

Don Stauffer

Leland & Barbara
Edwards

Ronald Holcomb

Harold & Winona Helms

Jack Hayford

Hazel Harry

Allan Lamb

Evelyn Thompson

Virginia Kindt

Jim & Marylou Ritch

Carl & Maxine Lucht

Helen Jensen

Jesus – "My dearest blood relation." A note from Harold brought great encouragement and comfort to us.

Hope Vollmer

When I think of Harold Chalfant, I think of so many things. At first, I must admit, I was a little awed by him, recognizing the fact that he was such a powerful motivator for the Lord.

Our first opportunity to minister with Harold took place when my late husband, Lester Vollmer, was the Sunday School Director in the Midwest District. Later, as we became Crusader Youth Directors in conjunction with our Sunday School work, Lester and I traveled with Harold visiting the churches and having him speak at our crusader Youth Camps.

We were amazed when Harold asked Lester if he would consider the position of National Crusader Director. We prayed about it and felt it was God's will for our lives. What an exciting life we had! Those of you who knew Harold would agree with me that life was sometimes overwhelming being around him! He could make the dullest day exciting!

It was inspirational to see God use a man who loved souls all over the world. He had them in his heart until the day the Lord took him home. The same vision that Harold Chalfant had was ignited within our hearts too.

Earle Williams

No one could create the excitement and expectation of blessings to be enjoyed in youth rallies, summer camps, missionary conferences or an unheard of train rally to match the fervor generated by Harold Chalfant. In his zeal to reach young people for Christ and challenge them to enter Christian service he set a pace of activities for young people that left little time for worldly attractions.

In the mid–thirties, I was given the opportunity, by Rev. William Nickerson, Pastor of the Burbank Foursquare church, to serve as the San Fernando Valley Crusader leader. Then in 1937, Harold Chalfant appointed me as Mountain Division Crusader Commander.

Carrying out the schedule of Crusader activities set by Chalfant was a plate–full! He always had something in mind for young people that was better, bigger or different than young people had done before.

In periodic leadership meetings Harold would present a challenge, such as the Santa Barbara train rally. All of us who were present in that electrifying meeting jumped at the concept and pledged our support.

During the weeks of planning, Harold spent considerable time traveling across the nation, holding youth rallies or participating in pastor conferences.

During these trips away, Harold wrote me letters of encouragement, admonition, challenge and supervision. His scribbled letters sometimes were hard to read but worth it. He made the work of the Lord the most important work I could do. His letters helped me make a prayerful decision to enter the ministry upon graduation from Bible College.

Upon my graduation from L.I.F.E. Bible College, Harold asked me to meet with him and Dr. Knight who said, "Harold has recommended that you come and serve as Angelus Temple Crusader Commander."

All this put me in touch with Harold almost daily – times of prayer, times of fun and times of planning which usually ended with another job to carry out. During my time at Angelus Temple and at Harold's recommendation, Sister McPherson appointed me as Vice Commander of the International Crusaders.

Harold showed me the big picture. He inspired me and challenged me to make a commitment to serve our Lord unhesitatingly. Eileen and I began part time in 1937, became full time in 1941, and have been, "over our heads" in the work of the Lord ever since.

KARL AND LEONA WILLIAMS

Harold Chalfant's life and mine parallel in that we were both challenged by the ministry of Dr. A. P. Gouthey, while he was preaching at Angelus Temple. We both graduated from L.I.F.E. Bible College in 1935. Harold became the first International Crusader President and I built and founded the Norwalk Foursquare Church. In Bible College we were both vitally interested in missions.

While I was pastoring, Harold took his epic never–to–be–forgotten trip to the Green Hell of Bolivia in South America. He was inspired by the dedication and courage of Jack Anderson and came back excited about reaching the Indians there. As he spoke at Crusader rallies and camps, his enthusiasm and dedication electrified young people to give their lives to the Lord.

Harold began the camping program at Camp Seeley, then Camp Radford, and finally at Camp Cedar Crest which was located and purchased. He became the catalyst in its building. During construction, we had a major part in building the Long Beach cabin as well as the Chalfant auditorium, and the infirmary, known as the Williams Center. His dynamic challenges at camp inspired young people to follow the call of the Lord to ministry and the mission field.

At Cedar Crest, we had the first men's camp emanating from the Long Beach church. As other church groups joined, this needed outreach for men grew. As a result, I was instrumental in founding the Council of Foursquare Men (CFM) . This inspired men from other districts across the United States to initiate camps.

LOREN AND DORIS WOOD

I first became acquainted with Harold Chalfant when I was 15 years old. I attended many of the missionary youth rallies that Harold conducted. It was at these rallies that I was deeply inspired to surrender my life to Christ for Christian service, The power of the Holy Spirit was so strong that the altars would be filled with young people responding to God's call to service.

In January 1936, while still in high school, I enrolled in L.I.F.E. Bible college to prepare myself for God's service.

Harold was one of our missions teachers. He took a very special interest in all of the students. One weekend he invited me into his home so he could deal with me on a personal basis of not only giving God my best but my all.

On August 26,1939, Doris Crane and I were married in Yuma, Arizona. Doris and I decided that we would spend our first day of married life at Camp Radford, so as soon as we were married we headed for Radford. We arrived at Radford just as the sun was coming up. The entire day was filled with the rich blessings of God.

Harold's life and personal interest in me never ceased to inspire and encourage me. While Doris and I were pioneering a new church in Springfield, Illinois, Harold would come by in his travels across the United States, It was always a joy to have him come.

When construction first began at Camp Cedar Crest my father and mother (Floyd and Inez Wood), were greatly involved. My parents lived in a tent at Cedar Crest. My mother cooked for the workmen and my father did the dynamite work blowing up the big boulders so that a road could be built from the camp site to the main road. Harold Chalfant has been a special friend of my parents for many years and they counted it a special privilege to help Harold in those early days of construction of Cedar Crest.

PART IV
IN LOVING MEMORY

CHAPTER 16
IN LOVING MEMORY

MY DAD

My dad, Harold Chalfant, really cared about people. To me, he was without a doubt the most generous person I have ever known. Whenever I expressed an interest in any of his artifacts, he would send it home with me. One time I asked him what had happened to a priceless icon he had – "Oh that." he said, "So and so admired it, so I gave it to her."

In later years when he worked for Ampex, he won a sailboat for top performance in sales. What did he do but turn right around and give the coveted prize to a fellow worker who enjoyed sailing.

Not only did Dad share his material things with others, but he gave unselfishly of himself. When he was in the hospital, he made friends with the doctors, nurses and patients on his floor. He knew each one by name and could tell you all about their family history. He was a people person with compassion.

In the natural realm, Dad loved all nature: birds, plants and animals. When we took long hikes together, it was amazing to see him name every tree, flower, bird and animal. In dad's last years when he was confined to his chair – he had a telephone ministry. Many people have expressed to me what his ministry of encouragement meant to them.

Dad always taught me to be just as kind and considerate to a waiter or clerk as I would be to the chairman of the Board. He often said to me, "Joyce, God has given me a love for the unlovely." He truly loved people.

My Dad, Harold Chalfant, was used by God in a mighty way in reaching many thousands of people throughout his lifetime.

I am so proud to be his daughter.

Joyce Chalfant Bevers

MY GRANDFATHER

My Grandfather, Harold and I, shared a beautifully unique friendship. Words cannot describe how much his life, his laughter and his unfailing love meant to me. My richly stored memories of Grandfather will last forever.

We enjoyed sharing our love through letters. Throughout my entire life we shared our feelings, our hopes and dreams through letter writing. Up until the time God called him home, we wrote to each other regularly. How I long for one of his letters today. He used to say to me, "Jeanne, someday we will be together forever, when we both meet our Maker."

My Grandfather's love for the Lord was an inspiration to me. Through joy, happiness, pain and suffering the Lord was his way of life. His strength gave me strength to always put my trust in the Lord. He often told me, "God has never failed me once." Oh, how I cling to those words, which are so true today! My dear Grandfather Harold Chalfant would tell me that I inspired in him a desire to live – if only he knew how much he inspired me to live! To live to the fullest and know the joy of laughter, love and kindness.

Grandfather, you'll be forever in my heart.

Jeanne Sligar
Harold's little Granddaughter

Harold Chalfant
March 18, 1913 – January 16, 1989

Today I'm going home, my Jesus I will see;
Today my pain is over, whole once more I'll be.
Upon this earth I've traveled, to places far and near.
To spread the word of Jesus, to souls that are so dear.
My walk has not been easy, there was pain along the way:
Sufficient is my Jesus, and in His hands I'll stay.
You see, my friends my Jesus, was always by my side:
In His trust, His love, His mercy, forever I'll abide.
And so this trip I make today, will be my last you see:
To Jesus I will journey, in heaven forever I'll be.
Take heart, my friends and loved ones, my suffering is at an end:
At last I'm home with Jesus, He was just around the bend.

Ben Bevers
January 17, 1989

THE FLAME STILL BURNS...
WHAT WILL BE YOUR RESPONSE?

What does it mean to live a life of true and lasting impact? Many believe that "being somebody" means a life devoted to amassing material wealth, attaining world wide popularity or achieving remarkable accomplishments. Yet more and more we are hearing from people who seem to "have it all" and yet find themselves still empty and frustrated.

Faye Dunaway, the beautiful movie actress, was attending a gathering of the rich and famous at Lincoln Center. A newspaper reporter asked Faye, "Are you happy?" She responded, "I grew up in a small Midwest town. I was taught the American dream. Aim at success and once you attain it, then you'll be happy. Here I am among all the famous actors and actresses in New York City, but where is the happiness?"

On another occasion Raquel Welch said, "I thought it was very peculiar that I had acquired everything I had wanted as a child – wealth, fame and accomplishment in my career. I had beautiful children and a lifestyle that seemed terrific, and yet

I was totally and miserably unhappy. I found it very frightening that one could acquire all these things and still be so miserable."

So what is worth pursuing in life? If all the rewards this world offers leave us still searching and lonely inside, is any kind of fulfillment possible for us? In a world given over more and more to despair, the life of Harold Chalfant may offer a ray of hope.

Those who knew Harold Chalfant would be the first to share that he wasn't perfect. He was no super saint with a high beam halo who floated through life three feet off the ground. He was very real, very human, with the attending flaws and faults that we all live with every day.

But the thing that made his life such a remarkable contrast to the frustration so many experience today was a commitment to a simple idea. This concept was woven like a thread through the tapestry of his time here on earth – life touching life.

Consider for a moment the personal impact this man had on so many different individuals.

- "Through the years of Harold's ministry, we were very close friends and I witnessed the depth of commitment to Christian service, to young people, to the missionary field and certainly to the Christ he loved. His sermons…were powerful challenges. I stood at his bedside just a few hours before he passed from this life and gave thanks to God that I had been permitted to know so personally – a divinely called man, entirely selfless and fully committed." – Clarence Hall

- "When I think of Harold Chalfant, I think of the word influence. He was fun! He was inspirational! He was dedicated! He showed young people that the life worth living was one dedicated to the cause of Christ." – Harold Jeffries

- "I had known about Harold Chalfant from a distance... but I was never close to him until Camp Radford. At that time in my life... I was devastated by my dad's death and depressed with grief. My self esteem dropped to zero. It boosted my morale when Harold paid attention to me." – Jim Ritch

- "Harold was present at Angelus Temple on the occasion of the premiere performance of the musical "Majesty". When the performance was over, Harold came to me and affirmed his sense of God's hand, not only present that evening but also upon my life. Needless to say, to have such a great man speak with such affirmation meant very much to me. I rise with gratitude to God for Harold's anointed ministry." – Jack Hayford

The truth illustrated in these recollections is crucial for us to grasp. The life of Harold Chalfant made a lasting impression not because of talent, position or force of personality, but because Harold himself had first been touched by the life of Jesus.

It has been said that Christianity is better "caught" than taught. Most people aren't brought closer to God by clever arguments, or dazzling performances, or even an encounter with the miraculous. For the most part our lives are changed when we not only hear the truth, but also see the truth, reflected in the life of a person in love with God. When Harold shared his vision for world missions, or took the time to encourage a fledgling pastor or singled out a scared and depressed person for some special attention people saw Jesus. Harold Chalfant impacted lives because he allowed others to see the character, the priorities, even the passion of Jesus Christ reflected in his life.

This book is full of the recollections of those who knew and loved Harold Chalfant. Sadly, those of us who never had the privilege of meeting him will never know the benefit of his friendship in this life. However, we can know the same Jesus whose love made Harold Chalfant special in our lives today.

In John 1:12 we are told, *"But as many as received Him, [Jesus] to them gave He power to become the sons of God, even to them that believe on His name."* How can we come to know Jesus personally? John tells us that first we must "Believe". Believe what? Romans 10:9–10 gives us the answer; *"...if you shall confess with your mouth the Lord Jesus, and shall believe in your heart that God has raised Him from the dead, you shall be saved."*

But there is more to becoming a Christian than accepting certain facts about Jesus. John tells us we must also "receive" Jesus. What does it mean to receive Christ? In Revelation 3:20 we read, *"Behold, I stand at the door and knock: If any man hear my voice, and open the door, I will come in to him, and dine with him and he with me."* Jesus stands waiting at the door of our lives, making His presence known to us until we invite Him to live with us in a deep love relationship. All we must do is accept His offer of a new life as a gift. The Bible tells us, *"For it is by grace* [God's unmerited favor] *that you are saved through faith; and that not of yourselves: it is a gift of God: not of works that any man should boast."* (Ephesians 2:8–9) When someone offers us a free gift, our job is to simply and thankfully receive it. If you have never personally invited Christ into your life, you may do so by simply asking God to forgive your sin and to give you the gift of an everlasting relationship with Him. You may wish to express this by praying the following prayer:

> Jesus, I come to you now just as I am. I believe that You died on the cross for my sins. I also believe You rose from the dead to give to me the gift of a relationship with You. Please forgive me for my sins, give to me the gift of everlasting life, and dwell in my heart that I might share Your love with others. This day I receive You as my Savior and Lord. Thank you for saving me. Amen.

The Bible tells us that the one who believes in Jesus will never be disappointed (Romans 10:11). Welcome to the family of God!

The story is told of President Thomas Jefferson and a group of other men having to ford a swollen stream on horseback. A man on the bank of the stream carefully looked over the group and finally asked Jefferson if he would take him across. The President was happy to oblige.

After crossing the stream another in the party asked the man, "Tell me, why did you select the President for your ride?"

The man replied, "I didn't know he was the President. All I knew was that on some faces was written the answer, 'No' and on some the answer 'Yes.' His was a 'Yes' face."

When people looked at Harold Chalfant, they saw that same "Yes face". But with him, the "Yes" was coming from a higher source than human self confidence. It was Jesus saying, "Yes. I love you. Yes. I can heal you. Yes. I can make your life a grand adventure." Harold Chalfant found a full and meaningful life by saying "Yes" to God. The people he touched saw that reality in him and said "Yes" to God as well. What will your answer be?

We pray that this book about Harold Chalfant will inspire you, as he inspired us, to accept or rededicate your life to the Lord, Jesus Christ.

In His love,

The Chalfant Memorial Camp Committee:
Leonard Harvey, Jerry Jensen, Allan Lamb, Roy McKeown, Dean Miller, and Don Stauffer.

I Shall Not Pass This Way Again

The bread that bringeth strength I want to give,
The water pure that bids the thirsty live;
I want to help the fainting day by day.
I'm sure I shall not pass again this way.
I want to give the oil of joy for tears,
The faith to conquer doubts and fears.
Beauty for ashes may I give away.
I'm sure I shall not pass again this way.
I want to give good measure running o'er,
And into angry hearts I want to pour
The answer soft that turneth wrath away.
I'm sure I shall not pass again this way.
I want to give to others hope and faith,
I want to do all that the Master saith;
I want to live aright from day to day.
I'm sure I shall not pass again this way.

Author Unknown

Destination: ETERNITY!